TERENCE CONRAN'S
DECORATING WITH PLANTS

TERENCE CONRAN'S
DECORATING WITH PLANTS

SUSAN CONDER

GALLERY BOOKS
An Imprint of W. H. Smith Publishers Inc.
112 Madison Avenue
New York City 10016

To Neville, Gabby and Boo
With thanks to Jasmine Taylor
and Anthony Ayling.

First published in 1986 in Great Britain by Conran Octopus Limited

Conceived, designed and produced by Conran Octopus Limited

This edition published in 1990 by Gallery Books,
an imprint of W. H. Smith Publishers, Inc.,
112 Madison Avenue, New York, New York 10016

ISBN 0–8317–2169–3

Gallery Books are available for bulk purchase
for sales promotions and premium use. For details
write or telephone the Manager of Special Sales,
W. H. Smith Publishers, Inc., 112 Madison Avenue,
New York, New York 10016. (212) 532–6600

Printed in Hong Kong

CONTENTS

FOREWORD

Plants and cut flowers have the power to inject colour and a sense of life into any interior. To me, they are as essential an ingredient to an environment as doors, windows and furniture. Plants and flowers are reminders of all that is natural; of the pace and time scale of relaxed living when embroiled in the stresses of city life; of the progression of the seasons when life is spent in controlled and quite seasonless environments; and of the charm and ingenuity of nature.

Of course, it is natural to be intrigued by, observe more closely and assess more carefully that which is new, whether a recipe, place, colleague or social acquaintance, but I totally lack that Victorian fascination for and quest of the eccentric, the unobtainable and the esoteric – so no matter how many weeping figs I see, I never tire of seeing one more, provided it is a good size, well grown, well presented and well tended. No matter how many florists, supermarkets and barrows sell bunches of daffodils in late winter and early spring, a huge mass of freshly cut daffodils in my office or home is always a source of pleasure.

With cut flowers, the regular replacement of a jaded display by a new one is a cyclical rhythm I have grown used to. With each fresh display of flowers – I refuse to call them arrangements, as they are never formally arranged in the traditional sense – my spirits, and the room, receive a refreshing lift.

Wherever a big bowl of flowers or large plant is placed, a focal point is created. Very often, their introduction to a room has a ripple effect: perhaps a tablecloth is changed in response to the colour, a chair or lamp moved to a new position, lighting dimmed, brightened or angled differently, or even another plant or bunch of flowers introduced for emphasis. By making you look again at your surroundings, with fresh eyes and critical faculties, house plants and flowers are doubly valuable.

Although I immensely enjoy displays of cut flowers both cultured and wild from my own garden, I do not for one moment claim to be a professional horticulturist, and am fortunate in that the well being of my plants is left to others. In this ignorance, I feel I am not alone, and far more people have plants than genuinely enjoy their ongoing care and maintenance. It is high time for non-horticulturists to 'come out of the closet', as it were, and declare that their interest in house plants is purely visual.

How to maximize such visual enjoyment, with the minimum of fuss, is the theme of this book, which I hope will be used as a source of creative ideas and a new, unconventional and guilt-free approach to using and loving plants and flowers in the home.

TERENCE CONRAN

INTRODUCTION

Above *Bunches of fat, ivy-wrapped
snowdrops, a vase of ornamental
alliums and another of freesias and
forced lilac make an unexpected,
unpretentious combination. Whatever
the cost or the scale, flowers in a home
should primarily be welcoming, and
secondly make a clear statement of
personal style.*

Right *Orchids, both cut and growing,
fill an entrance hall with intimations
of luxuries to come. Fake parrots add
levity and humour, to keep the orchids
from becoming intimidating.*

House plants and flowers are elements of interior design that can be changed at whim, to precede the seasons, reflect the seasons or ignore the seasons completely. House plants and flowers can add colour to a neutral-hued room, support existing colour schemes or provide unexpected contrast. House plants and flowers can provide focal points where none existed before, camouflage a bad bit of design or emphasize a good bit. They can fill empty spaces and, on a larger scale, separate one space from another or even create a new space. A small plant or posy can put the finishing touch to a desk or work surface, or brighten a bathroom shelf.

While some house plants are practically life-time investments, many are cheap enough to be treated as expendable. Fresh flowers, of course, self-destruct in a matter of weeks, if not days, and there is never any justification necessary for their replacement.

Being relatively cheap, compared both to other objects of interior design, such as furniture, carpets, curtains and paintings, and other of life's pleasures, such as theatre tickets, a meal out or even a good bottle of wine, house plants and flowers should be chosen and used with far more courage, imagination and even humour than is often the case. People cook and dress with flair and the attitude towards house plants and flowers should be equally courageous and flexible, filled with a sense of experimentation and a quest for personal style.

A home without house plants or flowers seems incomplete. People buy house plants and flowers because they look nice, make social events more social, and provide a totally harmless way of meeting the need for self-indulgence that everyone experiences from time to time. Some people find the horticultural side of house plants intriguing, but most would be happy if the plants and flowers looked after themselves.

The bowls of forced daffodils, hyacinths or tulips in winter and spring, a bunch of sweet peas in summer or of Michaelmas daisies in autumn carry a particular pleasure to those who lead urban lives, often without a garden or any view of greenery. A window box or windowsill filled with plants softens such harsh views out, but plants and flowers can soften equally harsh modern interiors. Though obviously furniture, carpeting and curtains help, plants and flowers help in a special way.

PLANTS AT WORK

Odd angles and curious recesses can result when houses are converted into apartments; stair landings are often too small for any human purpose but too big to waste. Filled with plants or flowers, these unwanted spaces become focal points. A large clivia in flower spilling out of a wall recess can be the modern-day equivalent of a baroque bust in a shell niche.

Use large plants as building blocks, to separate one activity from another – the eating area from the living area in a multi-purpose room, for example. A large plant ingeniously sited can act as a subtle bollard, preventing people from bumping their heads on a low corner of a staircase. In a very large space, indoor trees and large-scale climbing or hanging plants can create a room within a room. A comfortable chair, in a circle of weeping figs, becomes a wonderfully private retreat.

Bunches of dried hydrangeas add high-level interest, with a gentle reference to their freshly cut counterparts on the table below. Arum lilies are floral chameleons, fitting as comfortably into this informal kitchen as they do in the rather grand sitting room on page 13.

Plants and flowers can be used to confuse your perceptions of space. Indoors and out can merge together in the most glorious way if the room opens on to a plant-filled patio or balcony, or if there is an open, floor-level indoor border in front of a window made into a jungle of flowering and foliage plants. More modestly, massing plants around and in front of a windowsill brings the greenery of outdoors into the interior, or intimates a pleasant landscape outdoors where none exists. Camouflage is a form of specialized confusion, and flowers can camouflage a badly proportioned room, a badly plastered wall, or a dull piece of furniture. Plants and flowers can also provide privacy, reducing the need for curtains or blinds, and semi-privacy from other members of the family.

CONSIDERING COLOUR

Although plants and their flowers encompass the whole range of the spectrum, green is the core colour. It is the colour associated with nature, and is psychologically restful for that reason. (It is also scientifically restful. Eyes receive green light rays almost precisely on the retina, so there is no need to focus.)

The range of green in living foliage is very wide. The green of a new leaf is different from that of an older one. A green lit from behind is different from that same colour front lit. Whether a light source is warm or cold affects how a particular green is perceived, as does the texture of the foliage. The Swiss cheese plant's glossy, dark green leaves become white with reflected light; the crystal anthurium's velvety, dark green foliage

reflects nothing and remains deep and rich green. Green surrounded by white seems darker than that same green seen against a dark background. Rarity value affects appreciation of colour. Leaves are expected to be green, and are very much taken for granted, but green flowers, such as lime-green zinnias or tobacco plants, are considered especially beautiful.

Plants with multi-coloured leaves are fashionable, although they are weaker and usually more expensive than their all-green counterparts. Some variegated plants are handsome; the spider plant, variegated *Ficus radicans* and the variegated pineapple plant, for instance. Others, such as crotons, some *Begonia rex* hybrids and coleus, are hectic in colour and not in the least restful. These leaves often contain an incongruous mix of colours, bearing no relationship to each other or to the form of the leaf. In some cases, such as the yellow and green-leafed abutilon, the variegation is actually viral in origin. While the reason behind a variation in colour shouldn't influence one's perception of it, variegated leaves often look unwell. Variegated plants should be used with discretion, and juxtaposing variegated plants with each other avoided, as they all end up screaming for attention.

Plants with solidly coloured, non-green leaves also need special thought. The white leaves of caladiums have the charisma of pure green flowers – exotic and intriguing. A white-leaved plant in an all-white room would be stunning, and could equally well brighten up a dark corner of a richly coloured room. Used in mixed planting, though, the white leaves would look muddled and lost. There are very few design rules that can't be broken successfully, but on the whole, coloured foliage

needs isolation from other plants to shine and is difficult to use.

Flower colour is more fleeting, and can be used with more abandon. Still, it should take its cue from – but not be dictated by – the colour scheme of the room. Exact matches are as unlikely as they are unnecessary, since flowers tend to vary in colour within the individual bloom and also as they age. White or beige rooms can take any colour. In rooms of a distinct colour, there are several attitudes to take. One is contrast: bright red tulips in a Chinese yellow room; bright yellow daffodils in a fire-engine red one. Then there is repetition: scabious in a pale blue room; pink roses in a pink one. In multi-colour rooms, one colour can be picked out as the 'star', or several of the colours, or a starkly contrasting colour chosen.

White flowers are foolproof. Because white reflects all the light it receives, white flowers instantly attract the eye in a room filled with colour. However, when seen against white surroundings, 'white' flowers are often less than pure. White tulips are sometimes tinged with green; white delphiniums often have black eyes, and even daisies often have bright yellow centres. The thickness of a flower's petals also affects its whiteness. The white of a fleshy stephanotis blossom is opaque; that of a delicate *Iris germanica* is semi-translucent.

Mixed flower colours are a mixed bag. Some flowers, such as sweet peas and de

An extremely sophisticated display of floral and foliage forms. Arum lilies, anthurium spathes and velvety green leaves, and the thread-like foliage of Cyperus papyrus *combine to meet the stringent demands of a room that is both classical and contemporary.*

Caen anemones, grow in naturally harmonious colour ranges, while others can be disastrous. The whites, pinks and reds of commercially mixed carnations make a coarse trio. And colours in a bunch of mixed dahlias can border on the visually lethal. Roses should collude in colour but often don't. Florists' mixed bunches may contain deep blue-reds, salmon pinks and dead yellows. Personally mixed colours offer more possibilities and more memorable results. Easy combinations include different values of a single hue: pale blue African lilies and dark blue cornflowers, or bachelor's buttons. Complementary colours have a more startling effect: blue gentians and orange pot marigolds, or deep purple irises and bright yellow buttercups. Of course, colour combinations needn't be polite, and absolutely brash ones, if carefully planned, can be refreshing: fuchsia-pink nerines and bright orange montbretias are one example; wine-red wallflowers and vivid red tulips, another. Like variegated leaves, the more colours that are included in a mixture, the more risk of confusion there is, and the less powerful the contrast. This is especially true if each colour carries a similar weight and distribution. The end result *can* be pleasing – like a field of wild flowers – but it often helps to provide a soothing green background of foliage.

IN SCALE

All other things being equal, the larger a house plant is, the more impressive. A large, free-standing orange tree or an extremely tall glass jar filled with huge branches of flowering quince becomes a piece of sculpture. (An important point:

although height and mass are impressive in flower arrangements, giantism in flowers usually isn't. Huge, cabbage-size chrysanthemums and dahlias have lost their natural grace.) A great deal of false economizing occurs in the purchase of plants. The difference in price between a small plant of a certain species and one double the size may represent four or five years' growth, and that much care on the part of of a commercial grower. If you bear in mind the fact that the plant is unlikely to grow in your own home as quickly as it does in commercial cultivation, buying big is almost always the right thing to do.

With smaller plants and flower arrangements, there can be safety, or chaos, in numbers. A dozen African violets, packed tightly into a shallow wicker basket, is striking; the same number scattered around a room randomly is a muddle. Ten or twelve small plants in a mixed arrangement just might work, but pre-mixed plant bowls are usually disappointing, and a room with a dozen different small plants evenly distributed is likely to look like a half-empty florist shop. But whatever their size, it is always pleasant to be in close contact with plants and flowers. After all, sitting under a weeping fig is more exciting than looking at it from a distance. The smaller the plants or flowers are, the more important it is to be able to look at them closely. A tiny jug with grape hyacinths would be perfect on a bedside table, for instance.

Visual safety in numbers and symmetry: the conventional formal arrangement of a dining room is emphasized by floor-level plant displays, based on a pair of philodendron.

Multiples of a single flower make a totally safe and totally successful show, as long as the colouring of individual blooms is similar or, if not, compatible. Here, colour variations from one coneflower to another add interest, not confusion or discord.

LABELS

Although house plants and flowers have not yet suffered the indignity of being peppered with designer labels, certain ones convey status and wealth. This is nothing new; centuries ago in Japan, the little lady palm, or bamboo palm, was grown exclusively by the rich and powerful. Orchid plants in flower still convey wealth, although cut orchids have lost this elevated position, as they are now mass-marketed at popular prices. Extravagant formal arrangements of flowers carry the message of money loud and clear but, sadly, the beauty of the flowers is sometimes lost in the general din.

The cost of a plant or flower is completely irrelevant to its inherent beauty; a great deal of money can be spent on an ugly plant or flower arrangement, or very little money on a lovely one.

GOOD FORM

A plant's form will have developed in response to its natural environment. The Swiss cheese plant's perforated leaves help reduce wind resistance in tropical storms; the plump structure of cactus allows it to expand and store water in the rainy season; the vase-shaped rosettes of the urn plant and bird's nest fern collect rain-water, falling leaves and general forest debris for food. The form, colour and scent of a flower are usually related to attracting insects which pollinate the blossoms and ensure the survival of the species. However, none of these particular skills and purposes is useful in the artificial environment of a house. Unlike furniture, refrigerators or most other domestic objects – whose beauty comes, partly or wholly, from form following function – whether or not you like the form of a certain plant or flower is largely subjective. Obviously, those plants that do have a job to do in the home must have a form suitable for that adopted function; a sparse, narrow-leaved plant would not block out an ugly view, and a display of towering delphiniums on a dining-room table would obscure cross-table vision.

Much is made of matching the form of a plant to the interior decor of a room, in terms of historical accuracy; cacti in a 1930s-style living room or an aspidistra in a Victorian one are two examples. They may look superb, but it is easy to become too cerebral or scholarly, thereby excluding more exciting plant solutions. A spiky, gaunt plant might well reflect the pure, uncluttered lines of a contemporary living room, but a delicate, frilly fern might be just as potent. Anthurium flowers, too, would be suitably modern in appearance, but a bunch of mixed wild flowers would provide a very welcome contrast in the same room. Be sceptical of books or theories that treat house plants with the inflexibility of a Chinese set menu: there are no fixed rules.

High drama with house plants, and plays on space. A multi-stemmed Dracaena marginata *extends skywards, while a modest (but well pinched out) avocado plant is elevated on its own mirrored pedestal. A mirrored table plays more optical tricks with a single cut stem of cyperus and a dark-leaved clivia in the foreground. This room is a natural stage setting, for people and plants alike.*

PLANTSCAPES

A house plant, like an ashtray, can theoretically be put on any horizontal surface. Unlike an ashtray, a house plant can show its displeasure by dying. It is relatively easy to match a plant to its optimum environment, but there is a definite knack to making full use of its design potential at the same time.

Of all the elements of interior design, house plants and flowers are the most visibly affected by the passage of time and their immediate environment. Wood may darken imperceptibly over the years, and wallpapers fade, but a month, a week, or even a few days in an unsuitable environment can make a huge change in the appearance of a plant or a vase of cut flowers. From that point of view, glossy photographic illustrations of interiors can be deceptive. The photographer may hire the house plants and use them wherever they look best, regardless of their horticultural requirements: the beauty of an instant is given the illusion of permanence, when, in fact, the plants are returned to the hire agency at the end of the photographic session. To the untrained eye, these pictures can be depressing; other people's house plants, as seen in books and magazines, always seem so much healthier than your own.

The horticulturalist will take the opposite view from the photographer: put the plants where they grow best, regardless of the effect on the design of a room, or the people using the room, and don't attempt to grow certain plants if the

environment is less than perfect.

Most people's attitudes towards house plants and flowers fall between these two extremes. You might well go to the bother of hiring or rearranging plants for a special dinner party. And while it's unlikely that you would consciously sentence a gardenia to instant death in an unheated sun room in midwinter, you might well accept and appreciate the short-term beauty of a plant (even though, theoretically, it could live several years in a perfect environment) just because it is the perfect ornament for a special occasion. A brilliant pink anthurium will have a relatively limited life in a cool, dark hall, but the dramatic shape of its flowers, and the colour it adds, will more than justify the plant's brief existence.

In a room surrendered to plants, the pleasure derived from sitting in such an indoor jungle more than compensates for the loss of floor space. Both total commitment to plants and total ruthlessness when they overstep their allotted space are necessary.

Dining outdoors is delightful; dining indoors, in the presence of a tree, is almost as nice. Placing the tree to one side of the window and the tulips slightly to one side of the table, counters the formal symmetry that dining rooms, by the nature of their furnishings, so often have.

GENERAL CHECKPOINTS

As long as you are aware of the risks that plants face indoors, you can sensibly weigh up the horticultural pros and cons of putting a particular plant in a particular place. (Weighing up the aesthetic pros and cons is a far more subjective but equally important exercise that follows later.)

In any room of the house, heat rising from electrical appliances – televisions, washing machines, driers, air conditioners, refrigerators, and so on – can make life uncomfortable for temperate-climate plants, such as azaleas, cyclamen and forced bulbs. Tropical plants such as mother-in-law's tongue, philodendrons, variegated pineapple plant and prayer plant, for instance, may take the heat in their stride, provided there is enough humidity. But use shelving, or some other physical barrier, to deflect direct heat (especially from radiators) away from even the most heat-loving plant. Gas fumes and fumes from coke boilers can be lethal (although natural gas is less troublesome than coal gas): African violets, begonias, Jerusalem cherries and baby's tears are particularly vulnerable. More generally, rooms that are kept at high temperatures in winter will evitably shorten the life expectancy of temperate-climate plants.

Plants create risks as well as face them. House plants can be grown on televisions, stereos, priceless antiques and office filing cabinets, all of which are vulnerable to water damage. If you are meticulous this shouldn't matter, but if your watering regime tends to be rather casual then you should site your plants accordingly. A saucer can give a false sense of security; it has a maximum, not infinite, capacity. The higher up a plant is, the harder it is to water carefully and the harder to assess any damage from overwatering. (And the higher up a plant is, the less likely it will receive regular attention.) On a lower level, the weight of a large plant can permanently mark a thick carpet.

THE LOCATIONS

DINING ROOMS

Self-contained dining rooms tend to be warm and atmospherically dry, like living rooms, but less generous in space. Dining areas that are an integral part of the living room or kitchen will obviously have the same temperature and humidity as their host rooms.

Symmetry is often part of dining-room design, simply because of the central placing of a table and chairs. Plants can help emphasize this symmetry (and formality); a palm or the tree-like *Dracaena fragrans* in each corner would add visual height to a room dominated by the horizontal plane of the table. Plants used asymmetrically – a multi-level group of ferns and trailing plants crowded into one corner, for instance – give the room an informal feel. Whichever approach you take, make sure there is enough space for passage around the table when the chairs are occupied, and that there is clear access through to the kitchen.

Dining areas, as opposed to dining rooms, can be given a separate identity with plants used as boundary walls and

screens. Use a row of head-height climbers, such as grape ivy, in heavy terracotta pots with individual bamboo tripods or white wooden trellis work for decorative support.

Flowers are considered by many people to be as essential on a dining table as cutlery. The arrangement has to be low so you can see and talk across it, or very high so you can see beneath it. Avoid the formal flower arrangements which have a macabre similarity with those used at funerals. Likewise, the chrysanthemum, iris and carnation syndrome. Instead, try tightly packing a low, round wicker basket with concentric circles of baby's tears alternating bright yellow ones with green and then silver; remove them from their pots first, and fill any spaces between the plants with damp peat or compost. Or simply fill a white soufflé dish with hydrangea flower heads. Fill as many egg cups as you have with cut snowdrops and their grey-green foliage; display them in a circle on a circular table, or a rectangle on a rectangular one.

Don't be afraid to temporarily rob your garden for a dining-table centrepiece. Garden foliage and flowers can often be observed in more detail, and more comfortably, in the course of a leisurely meal than *in situ* outdoors. This is particularly true of low-growing plants, and those that are at their best when the weather is at its worst.

Cut flowers and dining tables are automatically paired. Keeping the partnership from becoming boring is a skill; here tulips, eucalyptus foliage and paperwhite narcissi make a refreshing trio.

Garden plants, thoroughly watered and carefully dug up with soil clinging to their roots, can be transferred to an attractive temporary container, put on display for an evening, then returned to the garden the next day. Established rock gardens offer especially rich pickings: clumps of pink thrift in flower; little alpine pinks for scent as well as good looks; white or pale blue alpine campanulas; and bright yellow gold dust and dark blue gentians. Very large clumps are lifted and divided as a matter of course every few years for the benefit of the plant – if you can time their indoor show with lifting and dividing, so much the better. Or you could turn out the contents of a window box and pot up the plants for a one-night stand on the dining-room table: trailing geraniums, *Helichrysum petiolatum* and lobelia can decorate a table as effectively as they do a window.

'Non-returnable' solutions include long sprays of ivy, Virginia creeper, honeysuckle, ornamental grape or perennial Scottish flame flower cut from the parent plant and brought indoors. Place the cut stems in a low bowl and let the greenery extend outwards in all directions over the table. On a smaller scale, use trailing stems of the pretty, golden-leaved creeping Jenny or silvery *Lamium maculatum* 'Beacon Silver', or arching branches of fishbone cotoneaster in berry or flower. A few sprigs of variegated mint or lemon balm can add scent and colour to a table for two; a huge, overspilling bunch of either will easily command a table for eight people.

If you have no garden, or even window box, but want something out-of-the-ordinary for a dining-room centrepiece go to a garden centre, instead of a florist, for inspiration (see page 35).

KITCHENS

Kitchens tend to fluctuate in temperature depending on whether the cooker (stove) is in use. When kitchen windows are opened to counteract the build-up of heat or steam, the temperature will drop dramatically. In large kitchens, one area may be consistently warmer than another – next to an old-fashioned oil or solid-fuel stove, for example. Humidity, too, fluctuates as steam rises from cooking and from hot washing-up water, but is generally high. Natural light levels tend to vary, depending on location, from bright and sunny to non-existent in internal, galley-like kitchens.

Space is at a premium in most kitchens and multiple demands are usually made of horizontal surfaces. Here is a case for fitting in modest plants for companion-ship and homely cheer rather than for high drama. Still, even a small amount of greenery is welcome, as it softens the sometimes clinical appearance of ceramic tiles and vinyl or stainless steel surfaces, and enhances the natural beauty of terra-cotta, cork, wood and marble.

Much is made of growing herbs in the kitchen and of course it can be done, but only on a regular replacement basis. Most

This kitchen window, sunny and subdivided by glass shelves, provides a satisfactory home for pot-grown specimens. Turn the plants regularly, to give them an even exposure to the light, and use utmost self control when harvesting the tiny crop, if the herbs are to remain attractive.

Left *A pleasant domestic muddle: high-level wicker baskets contain pansies and variegated piggy-back plant. The kitchen is rarely a place for grandeur or large-scale floral displays. Often, as here, plants have to muck in as best they can, with nearby equipment and utensils. Make sure high-level plants don't intrude on low-level activities or get in the way of drawers or cupboard doors.*

Below *Neatly set out rows of Boston ferns take advantage of the natural daylight on one side and the steam from the kitchen sink on the other. It takes a tidy mind to keep these shelves from becoming general kitchen catch-alls.*

popular herbs – rosemary, sage, thyme, marjoram, tarragon and bay – are of Mediterranean origin. As well as full sunlight, which they might well get on a sunny kitchen windowsill, they need maximum ventilation, a dry atmosphere and a cold winter rest period – which they won't get. Sooner or later the herbs become second-rate versions of their outdoor counterparts. If you have a garden or a kitchen window box, bring the herbs in on a rotation basis for a short stay. And remember that herbs continually being shorn of leaves do not make beautiful specimen plants.

Kitchen windowsills often become the *de facto* surgery, hospital and convalescent home for ailing plants and a place where new plants start life, as cuttings. Such mundane images are unlikely to be illustrated in interior-design books, but they are part of modern living. Review the plants regularly – don't let the windowsill become a mortuary as well.

You can, of course, take a more professional approach to the kitchen windowsill. Heat- and humidity-loving plants, such as variegated pineapple plant, queen's tears or Cape primrose can be lined up on the sill, up the sides of the window in baskets, or on glass shelves built across the window. Another option is to hang plants from an overhead steel or wooden track. High-level hanging plants can look wonderful, but make sure they don't overhang drawers or doors, or shelving to which you need quick access. Safe choices are the virtually indestructible spider plant, asparagus fern, grape ivy and devil's ivy, while the far more exotic, orange-flowered *Columnea* would get the high humidity it needs to flourish if sited directly above the sink.

BEDROOMS

Being able to see greenery from your bed is restful, even romantic. Conditions are often ideal for house plants: bedrooms are usually kept at slightly lower temperatures than the rest of the house and are unlikely to be draughty or full of fumes. Temperate-climate plants, needing a cool but frost-free environment, would find a cool, sunny bedroom comfortable and a good place for overwintering: Cape leadwort, pelargoniums, heliotrope and fuchsias are good examples. But because few waking hours are spent in the bedroom, plants here are the first to be neglected: they need to be the subject of a disciplined watering regime.

More than any other room, bedrooms are often assigned a gender – frilly, soft and 'feminine' or stark, domineering and 'male'. There are house plants that can emphasize the male-ness or female-ness of a bedroom. Hugely vertical cacti leave no one in doubt as to their symbolism. Plants of uncompromisingly rigid form, such as agaves, would be a more subtle, but still masculine choice. Plants with feminine overtones include anything flowering, fragrant or frilly, for example Boston or asparagus ferns, gardenia, jasmine, stephanotis, or orchids, all of which would be a pleasurable addition to any bedroom.

You can use night-scented plants, those pollinated by night-flying insects in the wild, to fill a bedroom with summer fragrance – window boxes or windowsills full of tobacco plants or night-scented stocks, for instance. If sun, shelter and space allowed, a huge pot of night-scented angel's trumpet would be heavenly under

a bedroom window. A bunch of violets or a vase of cut flowers in a guest's bedroom is a traditional gesture of hospitality and helps ease the stranger-in-a-strange land feeling of being in an unfamiliar house.

Whether very young children appreciate plants in their bedroom is a moot point, but if it makes the parents happy (and the plants are out of reach) that's reason enough. Older children often like to get involved in the tending of plants, especially those they can grow easily from seed or ones that 'perform', such as an avocado grown from a stone, or a spider plant forming a stem or a baby. Tiny plants, and collections of tiny plants, often fascinate small children: cacti and succulents are the usual choice, although African violets are equally suitable. Avoid carnivorous plants as they are almost impossible to keep alive.

Above *A cluster of diminutive cacti enliven a work space.*

Left *In a bedrooom, a small private jungle of ferns and a weeping fig emphasize the restful quality of the room, perhaps encouraging a Rousseau-like dream or two. In the context of a bedroom, the pots of cacti have their own, mildly amusing connotations.*

Hallways usually demand verticality, stability and large scale. A pair of Dracaena fragrans, *grown as standards, fit the bill. Standing sentry on either side of the entrance to a hallway, they combine symmetry with good sense, and the matching saucers protect the immaculate wooden floor from accidental spills.*

HALLS AND STAIRCASES

While some entrance halls are sunny, most are dim or artificially lit. And, generally, they suffer from periodic draughts and temperature fluctuations. Long-term plants may well be out of the question, although short-term, dried and artificial flora offer scope for creativity.

Halls are places of transition, never a final destination, so one or two tiny plants will not get the lingering attention they deserve. Instead, choose relatively large floor-level plants, which should be upright, stable and tough, and out of the way of opening doors.

Narrow halls often have high ceilings, and the double-height space where hall and staircase meet could be the perfect place for a potted tree. A huge, upside-down bunch of dried angelica or cow parsley seed heads suspended from a high ceiling has the grand scale and shadow patterns of a chandelier, with none of the pomposity. Large balls of dried flowers establish a pleasing rhythm hung from a narrow hall ceiling (if there is ceiling lighting, remember the fire risk and access to change the bulbs).

If you are lucky enough to have a wide curving staircase, and funding to match, in winter place a pot of cyclamen, azaleas or poinsettias on each side of every tread; in spring replace them with forced hyacinths or daffodils, and in summer with lilies.

Although the combination of cool temperatures and bright light are ideal for many flowering plants, cool, dim light can also be turned to advantage. The Victorians used the Ward case (a forerunner of the modern terrarium) to house a wide range of fragile plants. Inside its closed environment, humidity could be kept evenly high and draughts excluded.

Several ferns, such as the holly-leaved fern, asparagus 'fern', and even the hart's tongue fern, can be housed in a dimly lit hall without the protection of a terrarium, although they should be given several weeks in brighter light from time to time, if they are not to dwindle.

The Victorians managed to train ivy up the bannisters of staircases, with a minimum of fuss. Plants and staircase landings are predictable combinations, specially if there is a source of light nearby. A single, attractive chair often completes the trio, though there are few reasons to sit on a staircase landing. Try placing a large fern on a small bentwood chair, or several ferns on a couple of chairs if there is room. If large enough, brightly lit landings can be treated as small sun rooms. Some stairs and upper halls are lit by skylights, which can be used to illuminate plants, either in hanging baskets or on the floor beneath.

What can be achieved in communal entrance halls is more limited because little territorial instinct or pride-of-possession exists. Very nice plants run the risk of being taken, while those 'donated' are usually past their prime.

BATHROOMS

Bathrooms, like people, often suffer from stereotyping and images of small, ill-lit, claustrophobic rooms spring to mind. It is true that few bathrooms have large windows and, generally, privacy takes preference over light. If there are no windows at all, then the environment is

High-level interest

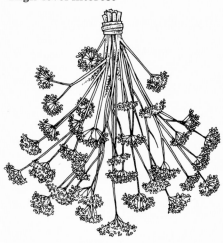

Dried flower stalks and seed heads of cow parsley, angelica, or other members of the Umbelliferae *family, look lovely hung upside-down in a high-level entrance hall. In natural silvery beige, or spray painted a single colour, the sculpture effect is that of a chandelier, with none of the expense or pomposity.*

A hall-like veranda ending in a plantscape. Ivy, aspidistra, ferns and palms create a mini-jungle, pretty to look at, and well out of the normal traffic route.

unsuitable for long-term plants, although they can be put there for short stints. Cut flowers, which are short-lived anyway, would be ideal. Some bathrooms are heated to much the same temperature as the living room; others are usually cooler, but a hot bath brings the temperature up and increases the humidity. Bathrooms are the most humid rooms in the house.

Most plants in a bathroom end up on a windowsill; plants and obscured glass make a sensible pair, the former relieving the banality of the latter. Dense plants and clear glass work well enough in the daytime but provide little privacy at night if the room is brightly lit. If you do opt for curtains or blinds, as well as plants, make sure you can get at their pull cords.

Because bathrooms are usually used by one person at a time, problems of circulation are minimal, so creating a Rousseau-like jungle here is less disruptive than it might be in a hallway or kitchen. Also, horizontal surfaces filled with plants cannot become cluttered with the tubes, jars and bottles that so often get taken out of the medicine cupboard but not returned. The top of the toilet cistern is a good place for plants, hanging or trailing if the cistern is high level, and small or upright if the cistern is low level. As access to the cistern may be necessary from time to time, the plants should be easy to move. Spider plants, asparagus ferns, grape ivy and foxtail ferns could put on a high-level display, while aspidistra or holly-leaf fern could provide low-level greenery. Avoid plants with spikes or thorns at any level.

If the ceiling is high, the space above the bath can be filled with hanging baskets. The plants benefit from the rising steam, and overwatering can cause no spillage damage: trailing philodendrons and ivies,

bromeliads such as tillandsia or guzmania; and epiphytic orchids such as cymbidium are all good choices.

If there is any free floor space, it is usually an odd corner, which could fit a tall vertical plant, such as *Dracaena marginata*, the umbrella plant, or weeping fig. Palms conjure up images of oases; other house plants with waterside origins include bulrush, grassy-leaved sweet flag, arum lily and the umbrella plant.

You can use the fragrance of real flowers to counteract the effects of disinfectants and room fresheners. Hyacinths or narcissi, are seasonal pleasures, while scented-leaved geraniums will grow all year round, given enough light.

Above *A novel approach to bathroom demarcation. Weeping figs, a Norfolk Island pine, yucca, fatsia and mistletoe fig line a glass wall. The effect is that of a suggestion of enclosure, rather than total privacy: perhaps not to everyone's taste.*

Right *Insufficient light and lack of obvious space are two usual drawbacks of bathrooms, as permanent homes for plants. Here, a skylight supplements the light coming from the window, and the fern has room to arch up and over the bath. Other, less obvious but equally suitable spots for plants include the top of a cistern or medicine chest.*

Above *Fireplaces are natural focal points. Here, a modest row of ivies, unvariegated but unapologetic, line a mantelpiece. The identical saucers are pleasing in shape, and become a feature instead of an eyesore.*

Right *A quite magical curtain of passion-flower foliage marks the entrance to a sunroom, and a complete change of flooring, furniture and pace. Infinitely more delicate and dramatic than more ordinary curtaining, this effect is unlikely to be long lived in a home with heavy traffic.*

LIVING ROOMS

A living room is usually warm, atmospherically dry, and the best room in the house, in terms of size and proportion, location and views out. It is usually the most public and communal room, too, where you can work and relax and where guests are entertained. Being the setting for special events and a functional place for everyday activities, it is the room where you are most justified spending money on plants and flowers. The living room sets the horticultural style and tempo for the rest of the house: a basic plant population, with extras called in for social or seasonal drama. Floor space is usually less at a premium in a living room than in other rooms of the house, so you could create a virtual jungle of intermingled tall, wide-spreading and creeping plants here.

A large indoor tree is never out of place in a living room, however small the room is. A sparmannia would look good by a sofa and a palm could fill a corner behind a diagonally placed chair. Large-scale doubles games can be played in spacious living rooms; a pair of weeping figs, placed either side of a sofa, will give it the stature of a throne.

The living room is also a good place to display small plants because you have room and time here to stop and absorb their beauty. A dense, lush collection of plants, such as a dozen pots of creeping fig or button fern, could provide a permanent background for more fleeting displays: three, six or a dozen hippeastrums could be incorporated into the greenery in winter, or the same number of marguerites in summer.

PLANT MAGIC

In the living room you have *carte blanche* with plants and flowers, and all of the ideas that follow are applicable. Many, of course, are equally effective elsewhere in the house. Choose those that suit your sense of style, available space, and budget, or use them as creative springboards.

CARPETS AND CURTAINS

Make a waterfall of greenery in an unused corner, with a large, central plant surrounded by a cluster of smaller, trailing ones. Or use an old-fashioned, multi-level plant stand to provide height. Give creeping fig, ivy, Swedish ivy, purple heart, arrow-leaf plant or wandering Jew (*Tradescantia* and *Zebrina*) its freedom to tumble down and grow a little way along the floor. Snip the plants back if they become too boisterous, and avoid large-leaved quick-growers such as *Cissus*. The lowest shelf of a bookcase or a low-level windowsill can provide the initial height for the display if there is floor space in front. Selaginella and moss really are like plush, green pile carpets (both do best in light shade, and need daily misting to thrive). Pack either tightly into large, shallow terracotta pans or round dishes.

Hanging and climbing plants can act as curtains, helping to provide privacy in windows, act as space dividers or simply as ornamental features. Like fabrics, plants can be practically transparent, semi-transparent or opaque. Hearts entangled, with its tiny heart-shaped leaves, is the equivalent of a lightly beaded

curtain; its presence is a delicate one, and little is concealed behind it. Use the florists' asparagus fern (*A. setaceus*), filmy and delicate, instead of a lace curtain. The popular emerald feather (*A. densiflorus* 'Sprengeri') has slightly less delicate foliage, and more of it, while the foxtail fern (*A. densiflorus* 'Meyers') is thick and dense. Hoya and stephanotis leaves are thick and opaque but spaced well apart, and although appearing quite dense and tangled when grown round the traditional wire ring, both plants have a much more open and airy feeling when trained up trellis work or wires. Ivy, grape ivy and *Cissus* give complete coverage.

The 'mother and baby' plants also vary in opacity and coverage. There are two plants commonly called mother of thousands: *Saxifraga stolonifera* and *Tolmeia menziesii*. The former makes its babies on long, thread-like runners of incredible delicacy, so fine that the plantlets seem to float in space. The runners are easily damaged, so use this plant where it won't be jostled. *Tolmeia* makes no runners, but carries its babies on the upper surfaces of older leaves. Although the weight of the plantlets eventually causes the leaves to hang down, no great length is ever achieved; the plant remains basically a ball of greenery. Spider plant is as tough as old nails and can provide a dense sheet of pale yellow runners, thick with plantlets and up to 1.2 metres (4 feet) in length. It looks superb on a shelf above a door for a dramatic entrance effect.

Open-plan living in fact is often less functional than in theory. Here, curtains of greenery help separate one activity from another.

Curtains up

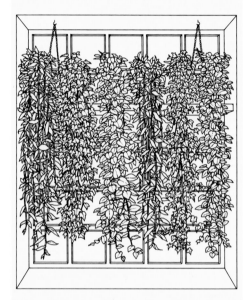

The Dutch have an attractive habit of displaying plants on window shelves throughout the year. For a more temporary effect, a simple plant shelf can be suspended from hooks in the window frame. In the summer months, pots of hanging and trailing plants, such as ivy-leafed geraniums, columnea, grape ivy and mother of thousands, could form a living curtain. Like net curtains, the foliage discreetly screens domestic life from the passing world outside, and perhaps screens less than beautiful views.

Choose plants with care, especially if the window is south- or west-facing (north- or east-facing in the southern hemisphere); summer sun can be very fierce. The plant shelf can be taken down for the winter months, and heavy curtains hung.

BRINGING THE GARDEN INDOORS

Even if you don't have a garden, there is nothing to stop you going to a garden centre for indoor inspiration. Hardy and tender outdoor plants can be used in any room of the house at any time of the year, provided you accept they are short term. The cooler, brighter and airier the conditions indoors, the longer the plants will last, but even if they last only a week they will have given that much pleasure. When choosing the plants it is worth looking to the past. Fashions in plants, like fashions generally, change over the years and old books on greenhouse management include dozens of examples of plants that are grown exclusively outdoors these days: maple, spotted laurel, bamboo, lilac, forsythia, camellia, spiraea, laburnum and even flowering cherry were displayed in pots and tubs in conservatories, and although the rooms were much cooler than today's centrally heated ones, the custom is well worth reviving.

'Working' garden centres (those that propagate plants as well as sell them) and nurseries often have greenhouses which are empty in the summer but are used in winter to shelter certain trees, shrubs and climbers – some of these are very nearly, but not quite, hardy, while others are perfectly hardy evergreens whose leaves tend to get discoloured by frost. New Zealand flax, yucca, cordyline, pittosporum, certain palms, evergreen clematis and evergreen Chinese jasmine are a few examples. These are the safest outdoor plants to try for indoor display and should last for months in a coolish room.

The cost of the display will obviously depend on its size, but many outdoor plants are no more expensive than a short-lived bunch of flowers. If you have no garden, treat the plants as expendable; if you have a garden, you can enjoy the plants indoors to start with, then move them out to a permanent position. In either case, keep the compost moist, remove dead flower heads, and mist the plants in high temperatures.

Ready-grown annuals are available from late spring onwards. Buy them in bud or, for more instant returns, in flower. One box of petunias contains more than enough plants to pack a brightly coloured bowl; use damp peat to make up the levels as necessary. In single or mixed colours, the flowers could equally well grace a formal dining table or a corner of a large work surface in the kitchen.

By the middle of summer, unsold bedding plants have become tightly crowded in their boxes, as each plant vies with its neighbours for space. Gardeners are wary of such plants – they are starved, drawn up, past their best and unlikely to continue flowering much longer – but the swan-song display of these bedding plants is often spectacular and, besides which, they are often sold off cheaply. Buy a few boxes for indoor display, just as they are. Their plastic boxes are inoffensive, but certainly not beautiful; remember that they are perforated and leak (a wrapping of aluminium foil would waterproof and conceal the trays). Occasionally, the plants are sold in slatted wooden boxes; if these are not too dirty, and the plants are dense enough to overhang the edges, leave the boxes as they are, displaying them on a cork or quarry-tiled floor, or on a wipeable table. Transitory, but charming. For narrow shelves or windowsills, transfer the plants into rectangular containers, again using damp peat to build up the levels. On the windowsill of an all-white room mixed bedding begonias, with their slightly coarse, candy-floss colours, or tightly packed dwarf ageratum will look more at home than they do in a garden.

Annual morning glories, black-eyed Susans, and, occasionally, cup and saucer plants, trained up canes or wires, are sold as 'outdoor' plants. Buy three or four of one sort and display them as they are on a low table, or remove the supports carefully and place the pots on a high bookcase so that the flowering stems can trail and tumble down.

If you have a garden, when frost threatens dig up as many healthy annuals or flowering biennials as you have space for indoors and pot them up. (Give them a quick spray against pest infestation first.) The annuals may go on for months in a cool, sunny spot; some 'annuals', such as tobacco plants and antirrhinums, are actually tender perennials and live in their native environment for years. In a warm, poorly lit room, the annuals might last for a week only, but it will be longer than they would have done if cut down by frost, and with annuals, time is always relative.

For those without gardens, late summer and autumn plants that you should be able to buy include pale-blue African lilies, bright-pink nerines and pale-pink or mauve autumn-flowering crocus. Bulbs in flower, such as these, are not cheap, and they do look most impressive in large clumps. But just one pot would cheer up a room a little, while half a dozen pots would make a bigger splash.

Even in the depths of winter, a trip to the garden centre will yield small treasures. Flower arrangers go to great lengths to keep cut Christmas roses from wilting, submerging the stems in hot water or pricking the stems to make tiny holes up the sides. Left intact on the plant, the white flowers, with their leathery green leaves as a perfect foil, should remain in good form for weeks. They are likely to be sold in a plastic flower pot or black plastic bag; you could transfer the plant to a terracotta pot. Small clumps of winter-flowering iris, such as the bright-blue *Iris reticulata* or the yellow *I. danfordiae*, would look wonderful in individual, glazed pots – the more iris-filled containers the better. Likewise, clumps of snowdrops flower at much the same time and white porcelain containers would show off the slightly green translucence of the flowers.

Hardy shrubs and trees are more expensive than annuals, perennials and bulbs, but even so they rarely cost more than a large formal flower arrangement from a top-class florist. A pair of weeping standard cotoneasters in berry would be splendid in an entrance hall or on either side of a fireplace. And there are several magnolias that flower on leafless branches; any of these, displayed in terracotta pots, would bring spring cheer indoors. Some, such as the star magnolia, are slow growing and so are more likely to be table-top size; others – *M.* × *loebneri*, for example – can be had as multi-stemmed plants of tree-like proportion for the same amount of money. The magnolias should be placed in front of a floor-level window, so they receive the light they need. Fruit trees are often less expensive for their size than ornamental trees, but are wonderfully ornamental when in flower or fruit. A pair of potted apple, pear, cherry or plum trees would be an intriguing temporary addition to a large dining room.

It is safest, and most seductive, to buy hardy plants in flower, but those bought in bud will give a longer display. With flowering trees and shrubs, make sure you can see fat flower buds; forcing totally dormant plants usually leads to the production of leafy growth rather than flowers. If you want the plants in flower for a particular event, allow two or three days in a warm place for the buds to open fully.

Timing the display of hardy plants indoors depends on several factors. If you intend to plant them in the garden afterwards, then ideally there should be a minimal difference between indoor and outdoor temperature. Of course, this makes winter the riskiest time of all but it is also the time when indoor flowering plants are most appreciated. To minimize the shock whenever there is a major difference in temperature, put the plant overnight somewhere halfway between the two; a cool but frost-free shed or garage, or even a cool bedroom.

People buy rootless Christmas trees without any qualms whatsoever, enjoy them for a few weeks until the needles drop, and then throw them out. The trees are expected to die, so they are used without guilt or reference to horticulture. Living conifers, with their roots still attached, offer enormous potential as short-term house plants; they can outlast potted chrysanthemums, and have far more class and rarity value. Whatever a conifer's growth rate, there is no problem about ultimate size if it is grown indoors because its container will 'bonsai' its growth.

Small conifers mimic bonsai plants at a fraction of the cost and worry. Young pine is very oriental in feeling, and Japanese

Left *Surreal and sculptural, a shallow metal container holds a tightly packed mass of mind-your-own-business, or baby's tears. On a less expensive scale, aluminium foil can hide a multitude of sins, from plastic flower pots to the shallow wooden boxes in which annuals are sometimes sold.*

Below *A scaled-down forest, with a garden centre as its source. Moss hides the compost and continues the forest theme. The basket makes the separate plants a visually cohesive unit, and protects them from the occasional accidental knock.*

yew, with its shiny, flat, leaf-like needles, looks far more like an exotic tender plant than a hardy conifer. As well as green conifers, there are yellow- and blue-foliaged ones. Ironically, these conifers are often misused in the garden in coy, cute or miniature schemes; indoors, without reference to nature, they can be displayed to advantage. A group of three conifers, in terracotta pots with the surface of the compost covered with tightly packed pebbles, would make an attractive feature on a polished floor.

OFF-SEASON SOLUTIONS

From late spring to early autumn is an easy time for indoor flora, especially if you have a garden. Annuals, biennials, perennials and many flowering trees and shrubs are at their best then, while cut flowers are cheap and the choice is wide.

During the period from mid-autumn to mid-spring things can be very grim indeed, especially without the resources of a garden. Potted chrysanthemums are cheap and cheerful but have the seasonal charm and reference of frozen beans. Christmas cherry, Jerusalem cherry and ornamental capsicum are in season, but the small plants have little real beauty, with their dull leaves and awkwardly upright shapes. Tiny azaleas, little more than rooted twigs burdened with flowers out of all proportion to their size and the size of their leaves, are actually ugly if observed with a very dispassionate eye. (Well-proportioned azaleas in flower and standard azaleas are quite another matter but so is their cost.) All of these small seasonal plants are best displayed in multiples, and

should be repotted in one larger container using moss to cover the surface of the compost. If you can't get moss, use pretty pebbles or washed gravel instead.

Cyclamen, senecios and slipper flowers have more natural grace and are easier to use as single plants. Even these, though, benefit from company, and a group of three or five of any one sort is bound to have more impact.

In the dark and dreary winter months, you can turn to a garden centre for more unusual plants (see page 35) including flowering bulbs. The traditional plastic circular bulb bowl sprouting three or four desultory tulips, hyacinths, daffodils or even crocus may not inspire much admiration, but there is far more scope for creativity. Slightly more unusual choices would be snowdrop, winter aconite, chionodoxa, grape hyacinth, scilla, dwarf iris. They are sometimes sold, two or three per pot, in flower though not forced.

(Garden centres have bulbs in flower all through the year, although they are more expensive than the dormant bulbs.) Take several flowering bulbs and decant them into a single large container. A rectangular glass aquarium can hold six or eight species tulips in flower; fill the space between the compost with large pebbles.

It is often more effective to have all the bulbs in a container the same, rather than trying to mix different types of bulbs or different colours of hyacinth, for example. The flowers in a mixed display might bloom at different times. There is one exception to the mixed-bulb rule: an indoor garden. Crocus, snowdrops and miniature iris, nestling in moss and lichen in a large container, is one possibility, but there are many others. The bulbs should be planted in informally arranged clumps,

Standard winter fare – azaleas, Christmas cactus, poinsettias, Christmas cherries or cyclamen – are most effective displayed in multiples. These cyclamen cheer up the garden, naturally dreary in winter, when seen from the inside, and cheer up the house when seen from outdoors.

Left *Place spring-flowering bulbs where they matter most, and can be observed and enjoyed at leisure: grape hyacinths and netted iris grow in small pots as a dining table centrepiece.*

Above *A pretty, non-matching collection of glass bulb jars allows the development of the roots as well as the leaves and plump flowers to be seen (an endless source of fascination). Older hyacinths that have gone floppy are best cut and their stems confined by a narrow-necked jar.*

as they would be (or should be) in an outdoor garden.

You should display flowering bulbs where they matter most. Hyacinths *en masse* can fill an entrance hall with heavy fragrance and brighten up a sombre hall table. Sweetly scented 'Paper White' narcissi would be equally good there or on a bathroom shelf. A small, sturdy clump of snowdrops might get lost in the muddle of a busy hall but would offer endless pleasure on a desk, to be contemplated between bouts of typing or study. Grape hyacinths are exactly the right height for a dining-table centrepiece where their slightly formal, soldierly habit of growth would not be out of place. Glass bulb jars for hyacinths are cheap and enchanting: stretch a line of them, single file, across the top shelf of a bookcase, down the centre of a rectangular dining table or in amongst the delicate greenery of a permanent collection of ferns.

LIFE AFTER DEATH

Those without a garden must expect hardy garden plants' lives to be unnaturally short indoors, but even in death, there is scope for creativity. Manufacturers of artificial trees often use a dead tree as the 'skeleton', on to which they fix artificial leaves and flowers. You can do the same. Dead birch, with its naturally weeping habit, is a superb beginning for an artificial tree, but any tree with a pleasing form is fine. Worth mentioning are the contorted corkscrew hazel (*Corylus avellana* 'Contorta') and the Peking willow (*Salix matsudana* 'Tortuosa'); both have curiously twisted branches – freaks of nature but fantastic instant sculpture.

While healthy living trees and dead trees both have design potential, dying trees do not. Once they begin to visibly ail, they should be put out of sight, if at all possible, until dead.

Composite multi-stemmed trees and shrubs can be made, using dead branches. Several stems of interestingly formed alder, oak or hazel, for example, can be massed together and set permanently in a concrete-filled pot. Although painting over the natural colour of a dead tree or branch might be considered akin to gilding the lily, don't dismiss its possibilities. A birch painted pure white, Chinese red or black is less natural but more striking than an ordinary one.

ARTIFICE

Nobody would prefer a rhinestone to a diamond, or a reproduction painting to the real thing. On the basis of absolute beauty, nobody should prefer artificial flora to the real thing: even though ever more convincing substitutes are being produced, living plants in their prime cannot be surpassed. Those whose interest in plants is purely horticultural might well find artificial flora repugnant and

Some plants, in death, have a beauty quite distinct from their living form: the horticultural equivalent of the difference between dried and fresh apricots, or dried and fresh figs. Here, a huge mass of bleached dried branches fills a brass tub, and another group of branches, more artfully designed, makes a low bas relief on the wall.

ironically, the more realistic it is, the more repugnant it may become. Some people, though, just cannot keep house plants alive, and find having to replace cut flowers too much to cope with. For them, fake plants are the perfect solution.

Artificial plants and flowers are made of silk, feathers, polyester, plastic, or various combinations, and, unlike other reproductions, are more expensive than the real thing. Why use them? Artificial flora needs no maintenance, except for the occasional dusting or wiping with a damp cloth. They can be bought and displayed at any time of the year. Combinations that would be utterly impossible with real flowers – summer roses and poinsettias, for example – become totally possible, if not plausible. Artificial flora never fades, sheds leaves or petals, stops flowering or needs replacing, however inappropriate or lugubrious the surroundings. Like stuffed animals, artificial flora is totally undemanding, but the amount of development and companionship it offers is nil.

You can approach fake flora in two ways: with an outrageously brash and jovial acceptance of its fraudulence, or by seriously attempting to mimic the truth. The second approach is harder to get right. Artificial flora made of plastic has crossed the line into kitsch, as have replicas of highly colourful or exotic tropical plants and flowers, such as crotons and birds of paradise. With these objects, the fraud becomes the message, not the original living plant that provided the inspiration. Also, familiarity breeds contempt: fake orchids, draping the counter of a local take-away restaurant, demean the real thing through overexposure.

The further away artificial flora is, the more convincing. Close observation re-

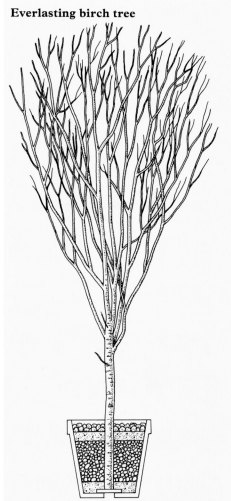

Everlasting birch tree

Cut off the trunk above the roots. Block the pot's drainage hole, then pour in a 4cm (1½in) layer of weak-mix concrete around the centred trunk. Fill to 5cm (2in) from the top with shingle. Check verticality, then pour a 4cm (1½in) layer of concrete. Top with pea shingle.

veals the joins between one material and another.' In living plants, the transition between thick and thin is imperceptibly gradual; in fake flora, there can be crude increases in girth, or none where there should be.

In the status stakes, artificial flora comes second to the genuine article every time. Whatever the skills of the manufacturers, there is still nothing like the real thing. . . .

On the home front, artificial flora is undoubtedly useful for spots where nothing will grow: internal bathrooms and kitchens, draughty, ill-lit halls, and so on. There is a risk, though, of transforming the personal and domestic feeling of a room into a depersonalized, commercial one, rather like a hotel foyer or restaurant, since artificial flora does tend to have these overtones.

The larger an artificial plant is, the more visual impact it will have, and it is usually better to splash out on one large plant than several smaller ones. Weeping figs, scheffleras, various palms and mimosa trees are all available in artificial form: often the foliage has been printed photographically to give a realistic rendition of the veins, midribs and undersides.

Because an artificial plant is itself a piece of fantasy, possibly the best way to treat it is to exploit the fantasy to the full. A 'mature' artificial banana tree, for example, might be vaguely believable in a sunny conservatory, but outrageously tongue-in-cheek, and effective, in a dark sitting room or internal bathroom. A wisteria trained as a standard tree is a rare horticultural treat; an artificial flowering one could effortlessly grace a bedroom the whole year through.

Artificial birch and willow trees and bamboo offer indestructible, evergreen company in the darkest, hottest, or draughtiest hallway. With these, the fake foliage is attached to the skeletal framework of a dead tree (or bamboo cane), so from a distance they are fairly convincing. Artificial standard bays or spotted laurel could be used indoors to flank windows or French doors beyond which living bays or spotted laurels grow. Some of these trees and shrubs are 'built' with more natural grace than others; make sure you choose a well-balanced, evenly leafy specimen.

Smaller artificial house plants suffer the same visual abuse or misuse as living ones. Mixed groupings need not be governed by horticultural considerations, but can look disastrous. Several plants of the same sort are usually more impressive and lack the overtones of 'airport lounge' gardening.

You could use artificial climbing and trailing plants, such as ivy, wandering Jew, peperomia and spider plant, to clothe walls and even ceilings with greenery. On a smaller scale, fill hanging baskets with them, again choosing a single sort and multiplying it as many times as necessary, rather than using a mix-and-match jumble. Or forget containers altogether, weaving the trailing stems round mirror frames or up the on/off cords of hanging light fixtures.

In nature, plant variegations range from the subtle to the frenzied. Variegations on artificial leaves are higher key to start with, and mixing variegated artificial foliage can be positively disturbing. Stick with all-green foliage, or those with subtle variegations of a single contrasting colour.

Finally, remember that plastic pots look even worse with fake plants than they do with real ones.

PLANT PROPS

Mirrors are the classic props to increase the drama of plants and flowers indoors, doubling the feeling of space as they double the image of greenery. In narrow halls, tiny bathrooms or above mantelpieces, the juxtaposition of flora and mirrors is a natural one. Shelves backed by a mirror make a traditional display case for collections – use them for plants or flowers. But a mirror used for a horizontal surface can lead to a confused double image, and unless it is kept spotlessly clean will look more than doubly grubby; the dish or saucer will also be reflected and may block out any image of the plant. Glass shelves are another matter; they let light through from one level to another and the plants seem to float in space.

'Props' can also mean things which offer physical support, such as bent wires, bamboo canes, moss poles and wicker poles. Circular wire frames need to be truly symmetrical to look good. As well as two-dimensional circles, try making a three-dimensional framework around which to train a small-leaved climber, such as creeping fig or ivy. Stick to simple shapes, such as cubes, cones, globes or pyramids, built out of small-mesh chicken wire filled with damp sphagnum moss. A single plant may take some time to cover the framework; quicker results can be had by planting several around the base.

There are less conventional supports. One plant can prop up another: ivy trained up a Swiss cheese plant or jasmine grown up a dead tree. Giving added height to medium-sized or small plants makes them more important and there are traditional pedestals and cache pots for the

Above *A trio of simple black plant stands, varying only in height, transform three modest peperomias into small living sculptures. Restraint in design is not necessarily synonymous with boredom.*

Left *Plants trained round hoops sometimes appear inexplicable; sometimes the hoop is off-centre, or the nature of the plant – bougainvillea, for example – is such that the plant actually looks uncomfortable. Healthy young jasmines trained round perfect circles are altogether different, and make superb accompaniments for a geometric marble obelisk.*

purpose. Whatever props you use, make sure plants at the lower level have access to adequate light.

Architectural details can be used as three-dimensional frames for plants. The grate and hearth of an unused fireplace is a traditional setting for massed shade-loving plants, such as ferns and ivies. With their naturally darkened surroundings, the plants would become doubly dramatic if spotlit. Recessed windows can act as visual frames; if the view out is unbearable, a white translucent blind would block the view and still allow light to reach the plants.

Use a whole wall as a prop to create an indoor garden. Walls with natural, rough surfaces – brick or stone – are more suitable than plastered or wallpapered ones. Either provide discreet wire and vine eyes, exactly as you would do for a garden wall, or make a positive feature of trellis work, using traditional diamond- or square-patterned trellis, mounted on battens. Whichever method you use, leave a space of 2.5 centimetres (1 inch) between the wall and the support system, so air can circulate around the plant, and the plant has space to twine. Do think carefully about the support system before you fix it because it is a major repair job to put right if you decide to take it down. The framework can go from floor to ceiling to cover an entire wall, giving the plants the role of wallpaper. A panel of wire or trellis work can be fixed to a narrow end wall or column, to create a vertical panel of greenery. Plants with tendrils, such as passionflower, grape ivy and *Cissus*, will make their own way up and through the framework, but it is no trouble training a jasmine, hoya or asparagus fern to the support system with the help of a few plastic-coated ties. In large rooms, free-standing open-work screens can provide props for climbing plants and a space within a space at the same time. The screens can be made of conventional trellis work strengthened with cross-pieces, or they can be purpose built. Whatever the material and style, the screening should be bolted to the floor.

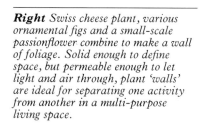

Right *Swiss cheese plant, various ornamental figs and a small-scale passionflower combine to make a wall of foliage. Solid enough to define space, but permeable enough to let light and air through, plant 'walls' are ideal for separating one activity from another in a multi-purpose living space.*

Far right *Lilies and oak leaves below, and mistletoe above, make an unlikely but lovely setting for a portrait of an Edwardian lady. Not quite* trompe l'oeil, *the effect is a slight play on space nonetheless, giving the two-dimensional painting a vaguely three-dimensional quality.*

SPECIAL DISPLAYS

Horticultural shows are unpredictable but excellent sources of plants for short-term indoor display. The commercial exhibitors present every one of their plants in top form, and often sell them at the end of the show rather than transport them back to the nursery. The last day of a major show is a hunting ground for devout gardeners, but it also offers rich pickings for anyone looking for indoor plants. You should be able to find unconventional plants – huge clianthus, medinella, standard wisterias, pyramid fuchsias or lovely, old-fashioned standard weeping roses – as well as bulbs in flower which are usually available only in their dormant state – tall-stemmed, bright-orange gloriosas, for example, or the eccentric pineapple flower. Many of the cut flowers will have two or three days of beauty left.

Christmas is always an occasion for showing off. While the traditional language of decoration – Christmas trees, wreaths, bunches of mistletoe, and holly and ivy decorating picture frames – is perfectly valid, there are more exciting options. Try decorating a weeping fig with clear glass Christmas tree balls, or cluster silver balls, like seasonal fruit, under the fronds of a palm tree or the rosettes of a multi-stemmed *Dracaena marginata*.

A standard orange tree could bear masses of out-of-season 'fruit' – multi-coloured Christmas balls. Give a smaller house plant a festive feeling by putting it in a large glass container and filling the space between its pot and the glass with Christmas tree balls. Buy six ivies trained up bamboo canes (those sold outdoors at a garden centre are invariably cheaper and

Berries and fruit are often overlooked as a source of transient interior colour, though they are usually at their best when garden flowers are few and far between. Here, rose hips, hawthorn, cotoneaster, pyracantha and mistletoe display their autumn finery. Very little 'arrangement' is needed to make these just-cut branches eminently presentable indoors.

Monkey puzzle is an awkward-looking tree, never really at home outside its native South America. Here, two branches have been transformed into an unconventional Christmas wreath, to adorn a simple wooden door. The moral: never dismiss plant material as unusable without experimenting first.

larger than those sold as 'house plants') and transfer them to terracotta pots sprayed white or red. Put the ivies, single file, on a mantelpiece or in front of a mirror on a narrow hall table. Brightly variegated ivies will need no embellishment, but you could add small red and white satin bows to pep up dark green ivy.

The Christmas season is the time to go wild with evergreens and berries, filling every available corner and container with as much as possible. As well as big branches of holly and tree ivy, both in berry if possible, use other broad-leaved evergreens: Mexican orange, bay, Portuguese laurel, laurustinus, mahonia, *Garrya elliptica*, and the strawberry tree. Try big branches of pine – their grey needles enliven the dark green of most other evergreens – or blue spruce, if you can get it. (Cypress and false cypress are unsuitable; both have a terribly mournful appearance. Yew is sombre in colour and connotation, too.) To make the evergreens more specifically 'Christmas', add a few stems of artificial white poinsettias; the leaves of real poinsettias are nondescript and their habit of growth naturally gawky, so both the poinsettias and evergreens benefit mutually.

Instead of the traditional Christmas tree, usually Norway spruce, a container-grown cedar or blue spruce makes an exciting alternative. For small, table-top Christmas trees, a trip to the conifer section of a garden centre should yield equally interesting possibilities. With winter foliage of bronze or reddy purple, a small Japanese cedar hung with gold and silver Christmas balls would be memorable. Or decorate a painted tree with ribbons and balls of a suitably contrasting or cleverly clashing colour.

Christmas spirit

Wrap floral foam with chicken wire in a globe shape. Firmly insert one end of a dowel, and insert the other end into a pot. Tightly pack with gravel. Push holly twigs into the globe and gravel, and decorate the dowel with ribbons. Mist the leaves regularly.

Left *Containerized garden plants can be brought indoors for 'one-night stands'. Here a shaggy bay tree is dressed up for a formal occasion.*

Right *Carefully placed back lights and front lights will add drama to both flowers and plants.*

LIGHTING PLANTS

Consider lighting for plants and flowers within the context of room lighting as a whole. Although high drama can be wonderful, it is not the only possibility. Often, a south- or west-facing room streaming with natural daylight (north- or east-facing, in the Southern Hemisphere) is the nicest possible way to present plants. Remember, too, that not all artificial lighting meets the plants' horticultural requirements, and that the plants themselves would usually prefer to be as close as possible to a window.

A plant-filled corner lit from below and behind by a baby spot, to create diffuse shadows and patterns of light, becomes an automatic focal point, as does a large bunch of dried flowers backed by a recessed mirror and lit from one side. Or try diffused, soft back lighting for a large, dense, plant grouping, combined with one or two narrow beams of a spotlight from the front. For real theatre, run a string of tiny white fairy lights, such as those used for Christmas trees, up and through the foliage of a weeping fig, huge dracaena or pyramid bay.

Dinner parties often tend to be ritualized, even ceremonial events, inviting a sense of theatre. Strong, intense downlights could accent a group of plants or single palm in one corner of the room, while a ring of candles round a floral centrepiece would sparkle in the otherwise subdued light. Glossy leaves and thick leaves with attractive patterns or textures are best displayed when strongly lit from above, in front or the side: when lit from below, it is the leaf undersurfaces that catch the light. Some plants have leaves with beautifully coloured or tex-

Scaled-down theatrical lighting, directed at the highly reflective container, illuminates the corner of a room. The intricate tracery of the dried branches is empasized against the golden light.

tured undersides: *Philodendron* 'Burgundy' has deep-red leaf undersides, as does the homely mother of thousands (*Saxifraga stolonifera*). The leaves of loquat and some rhododendrons have russety brown velvet undersides, and those of other rhododendrons have pure white felted undersides. All of these can be lit from below to accentuate what would normally remain hidden. The plants should be placed at eye-level or above for the best effect.

Foliage that is strongly lit from behind behaves according to its thickness. Thin leaves become translucent and can be intensely beautiful, especially when they overlap one another (but are least able to cope with harsh direct sunlight). Thicker-leaved plants become dark silhouettes against the light and the detail of the individual leaves is lost. Foliage that is indirectly lit from behind – for example, from light reflected off a white wall – appears less dramatic, with more subtle and more diffuse patterns of light and shade.

Generally the closer the light source is to a plant the larger and more dramatic the shadows, except for downlights directly above, which create minimal shadow. The closer a light source the more danger there is of heat scorching the leaves. An exposed bulb always causes glare and should be avoided if possible. The more flexible lighting is in a room – dimmers, electrical outlets, angled lamps, lighting tracks with movable fixtures – the more possibilities of experimenting. Don't be afraid to move a plant for an evening to display it in the most dramatic light; a mundane pot of chrysanthemums placed directly under a Japanese paper lamp-shade can be a temporary, one-night star.

POTTED PLEASURES

The relationship of a plant to its container is a multi-faceted one, involving design and horticultural considerations. As well as looking comfortable with each other, a plant and its container should both fit comfortably in the larger setting of the interior.

To horticultural purists, the purpose of a pot is to provide the best possible growing conditions for the plants, and not to compete with the plant for attention. To designers, the visual quality of a container is far more important, and as much thought is given to it as the plant itself. It is easy though to have the best of both worlds; there are containers that meet both high standards of design *and* horticultural requirements.

BASIC POTS

Most plants are sold in plastic pots, which, being lightweight, can be moved and stored without difficulty. Plastic pots are cheap to produce, rarely break if they are dropped, and, because they are non-porous, are easier to clean and sterilize than clay ones. Plants in plastic pots also need less frequent watering.

In the home, these commercial considerations become less important. Orange-brown, rimmed plastic pots, masquerading as terracotta, or unnatural shades of green, coyly attempting to con-

ceal themselves among the leaves, always ring untrue. Plastic pots moulded to simulate Renaissance stonework, yet with the thinness and weight of paper, are as aesthetically disastrous.

Traditional terracotta pots are much nicer and more permanent in feel. Terracotta is a heavy material, but a natural one, and is more empathetic to the natural form and 'fabric' of a plant. The weight of terracotta can be an advantage too: tall-growing plants with relatively small root systems can keel over or be knocked over when grown in small plastic pots and lightweight peat compost.

Five minutes spent transferring a plant from a plastic to a terracotta pot is money and time well spent. Remember, though, that not all terracotta pots are well designed. What is pleasing about the traditional 'flower pot' is the simplicity of shape, brevity of detail and clarity of

Never assume that a plant has to remain in the container in which it is sold. This exquisite display depends for its beauty on the containers as much as the orchids.

proportion and line, as well as the material. More elaborate pots, with Italianate garlands or putti heads, can be pleasing in the right surroundings too, but some terracotta pots are made with mean proportions, others have far too much decoration encrusting the surface or inexplicable squiggly lines. Sometimes, the design differences are more subtle; two terracotta pots may have the same height and diameter, but the curve from the base to the rim of one pot is more fluid and graceful than the other. How a material is handled, as much as the material itself, affects the quality of design. True connoisseurs of terracotta tend to prefer old, hand-made pots, always slightly asymmetrical and each one unique. Modern hand-made pots are available also, but they can be over-decorated, with prices to match. Factory-made pots are perfectly symmetrical and acceptable, but their colour is often a rather harsh, shiny orange.

Most plastic and terracotta pots are manufactured in standard sizes; they are measured across the inside diameter at the top of the pot, and the depth usually equals this diameter.

If you are displaying a plant in its pot, without further ado, provide a saucer or dish to catch any water leaking from the drainage holes. A pot placed directly on a carpet or wooden floor is asking for trouble; even cork, stone or quarry-tiled floors can be stained by water and by salts leached out of the pot and compost. Moisture will penetrate an unglazed terracotta saucer, defeating the whole exercise. Make sure that any saucer used has a flat base large enough for the bottom of the pot to sit steadily, and a rim deep enough to retain overflows.

Victorian cache pots, complete with matching pedestals, can be lovely in their own right. Usually of glazed pottery and varying from simple to rich in ornamentation and colouring, traditionally they held potted Boston ferns, aspidistras or trailing ivy. Sited in an entrance hall, living room or dining room, plant-filled cache pots become major focal points, possibly needing special lighting (see page 51). Unfortunately both genuine and reproduction cache pots and pedestals tend to be expensive.

Left *This selection of indoor plants – outdoors for a summer 'vacation' – shows the wide range of terracotta pots that is now available.*

Below *An old-fashioned bathroom with an old-fashioned pedestal and cache pot. Cache pots conceal less attractive containers, and prevent drips.*

WATERTIGHT CONTAINERS

You can plant directly into a watertight container, rather than a conventional flower pot with drainage holes, but you must be very careful about overwatering. Plants that grow naturally by the water's edge, such as the grassy leaved sweet flag and the umbrella plant, are quite happy in waterlogged compost but most other plants are at risk.

In the short term, for a special evening or weekend perhaps, you can transfer plants to decorative watertight containers, then move them back to their original pots afterwards. If you are using a watertight container for permanent planting, place a thick layer of gravel, mixed with a little charcoal, in the bottom of the container; top this with a thin glass fibre mat to prevent compost clogging the gravel, then finish with a layer of peat-based compost, again with a few lumps of charcoal added to keep the compost 'sweet'.

If you'd rather risk the container than the plant, you can drill drainage holes in the bottom. Use a masonry or wood drill for ordinary terracotta containers. Never drill a container you are not prepared to lose, and remember that if the object is a valuable one, even if drilling were successful, it would destroy its value.

When planting in a watertight glass container, camouflage the compost by building up a 'wall' of moss or gravel to line the sides of the glass; wet compost, clinging to the glass, is very unattractive. Gravel-filled glass containers are ideal for forcing bulbs; their immediate food supplies are stored within the bulbs, and no additional nutrients are needed.

Above Contemporary equivalents of cache pots, these empty food tins provide a home for plants and cut foliage. With the exception of the tiny orange berries of the bead plant, the traditional source of colour is reversed.

Right Usually the growing medium is the least attractive aspect of house plants; here it is a pleasing, 'geological' feature, allowing the normally hidden development of roots and shoots to be observed and enjoyed.

TROUGHS AND TUBS

Planting troughs filled with large plants are often used in offices to subdivide space or to define areas of circulation or seating. In the home, plants and troughs can do the same work, though very large planting troughs can have an impersonal feeling, recalling an airport lounge or entrance hall of a civic building.

A row or cluster of large terracotta pots filled with loam-based compost and tall plants is more homely and may be a better solution. Or you could try a row of wooden 'Versailles' tubs. In traditional glossy white, pitch black, or painted to match the decor of the room, the tubs would be attractive if filled with weeping figs or young jacarandas. Aluminium cube planters are available in kit form; and bamboo and rattan planters inevitably have oriental overtones.

Don't dismiss troughs sold for outdoor use; they can be equally beautiful indoors. If floor loading allows, reconstituted stone troughs, either resting on the floor or on stone supports, would be superb filled with ivy trained up poles and tumbling over the sides.

There are many materials to choose from: stone and reconstituted stone, wood, glass fibre, lead, plastic, iron, bamboo and rattan. Avoid mock finishes: plastic masquerading as wood or bamboo, or even as stone. Glass fibre masquerading as lead is an exception; it is a successful deceit because the finished surfaces and thickness of the two materials are similar.

Built-in planting troughs can look wonderful. A raised brick planting bed in a brick-floored sun-room, or a raised bed with a tile finish in a tile-floored room, are

Above *Movable stands make good sense in terms of design and horticulture. Sun-loving subjects can be shifted to take full advantage of daylight, and changing the position of the stand is not a physically impossible task.*

Right *Built-in planting areas can be immensely exciting, as here, but the concept should be approached with caution. Once built, they are there forever, as is the ongoing commitment to the contents.*

two possibilities. The beds are there for ever, though, and if you tire of them, or wish to change the layout of the room, removal will be an expensive exercise. Planters and troughs fitted with castors are infinitely mobile, and can be moved from window to window, so the plants receive maximum sunlight; wedge the castors once the planter is in place, or it may be more mobile than you intend.

DISPLAYING EPIPHYTES

In botanical gardens and large conservatories, epiphytic plants, such as bird's nest fern, orchids and bromeliads, are often displayed as they grow in the wild: attached to the branches or trunks of huge trees, either living or dead. Epiphytes are not parasites: they use the plants on which they grow for support, not food, and are as happy clinging to damp rocks as to trees. Epiphytes obtain nutrients from the decomposing plant and animal debris that collects round their roots or leaf bases.

You can use the same dramatic approach for displaying epiphytes in a home, although the larger the tree, the more difficult to accommodate and stabilize. In addition, most epiphytes need a damp atmosphere in warm temperatures and frequent misting in spring and summer. A more realistic option would be a large piece of driftwood, resting on a tiled floor or low table, with various epiphytic plants – their roots packed in damp peat-based compost and then wrapped in sphagnum moss – attached with fine wire or plastic thread.

You can make artificial epiphytic poles. However, their rigidity has little resemblance to the natural growth of a tree.

INDOOR WATER GARDENS

Most large-scale water displays indoors are sterile, with algicide keeping the water clear, clean and lifeless. While artificial pools outdoors can be ecologically balanced, with exactly the right number of fish and oxygenating plants for the volume of water, this can only be achieved in the presence of strong sunlight. Indoors, there is never enough natural light to support the healthy growth of aquatic plants, such as water lilies and oxygenating plants, except in glass-roofed conservatories or greenhouses. Theoretically, artificial light could replace sunlight, but the light would have to be so close to the plants that the object – to create a natural water garden indoors – would be defeated. A standard tropical aquarium, with artificial lighting enclosed in a hood, is a mundane but realistic approach. The aquatic plants receive all the light they need, and the water is kept clean by filters and air pumps.

A 'waterside' garden, with plants grouped round a sterile body of water, is worth trying indoors. As with permanent planting troughs, built-in water gardens are major commitments, lasting as long as you live in that particular house. The plants could conceal the sides of the container and also benefit from the humid atmosphere created by the pool. But remember that water is heavy – 4.5 kilogrammes per 4.5 litres (10 pounds per gallon) – and a pool with water more than 15 centimetres (6 inches) deep spread over a large surface can pose a serious threat in a house with wooden floor joists. A basement or ground floor might be safe, but in

The intensity of natural light indoors is insufficient to grow water lilies, unless 'indoors' happens to be a greenhouse or conservatory. Also, in a tank this small, a pump and filter would be essential, if the water is not to become stagnant. The image, though, is exquisite, and for those with water lilies and tanks to spare, the idea of such indoor, temporary decoration is worth considering.

any case always consult a surveyor or architect first. You will need to install a drain for disposing of dirty water, while a source of clean water should be close by.

A single or double row of bricks could be stacked round the pool, to conceal the sides, providing the floor can take the weight of the bricks. Of course, the bricks could be toppled by young children – but if there are young children in the home, a pool is an unacceptable safety risk in any case. Filters and pumps should be installed by an electrician and their presence concealed by overhanging plants. Check the noise level of a pump motor before buying it; some can be very noisy. Spotlighting a pool from above is more realistic than underwater lighting, except for the largest pools.

Garden centres or water garden specialists sell glass fibre and rigid plastic pools, reconstituted stone fountains and bird baths, both free-standing and wall-hung. Formal geometric shapes seem better suited to the formal geometry of domestic architecture than curiously irregular pools. Artificial pools outdoors are usually best when dark grey or black – the electric blue promoted as the natural colour of water is anything but – and although with water indoors there is no pretence of being natural, dark colours are a better choice.

On a smaller scale, you could install a wall-hung reconstituted stone scallop shell, sink or shallow bowl. Again, remember the weight problem, and avoid unnatural colours.

THE GROWING MEDIUM

The vast majority of house plants spend their lives in the compost in which they are sold. While most people have no interest whatsoever in the various types of compost available, if you do have occasion to move a plant into a larger pot or want to try plant propagation, it is worth knowing about the two main types of compost.

Commercial growers prefer peat-based compost, made largely of peat with added fertilizer and, sometimes, vermiculite, perlite or coarse sand. Peat-based composts are standardized, lightweight, easy to use with specialized commercial watering systems and less 'messy' than loam-based composts. On the minus side, they run out of nutrients quickly, since peat has none of its own, and supplementary feeding is necessary quite soon after potting. In addition, peat-based composts dry out fast and, once bone dry, can't quickly re-absorb water. Being lightweight, they also offer little stability for large, top-heavy plants.

Loam-based compost is made largely of sterilized loam, with peat, coarse sand or grit, fertilizer and ground limestone added. There are various proprietary brands available.

Loam-based composts are less temperamental about water-absorption than peat-based ones, dry out less quickly and contain more nutrients. They are relatively heavy, so offer stability to large plants and those in plastic pots. Most experts would advise loam-based compost for the amateur gardener, with extra peat or grit added for plants that require perfect drainage.

Garden soil is fine in the garden, but disastrous indoors. Very few soils are ideal loam, and even ideal loam would need sterilizing to kill pests and diseases, testing and any imbalance corrected, and the addition of peat.

REPOTTING

Assuming that you buy a reasonable-size plant, not a seedling or rooted cutting, the initial potting up will have been done already by the grower. You should move the plant to a bigger pot, if its original pot is too small, in spring. But if the plants are in flower or bud do not disturb them; wait until the display is finished. Roots growing through the drainage hole or massed on the surface of the compost are usually signs that the plant needs a bigger pot. Clivia and hippeastrum, however, prefer pot-bound conditions and won't flower in lush ones. To check the plant's roots, knock the side of the pot against a hard surface to dislodge the root ball; turn the pot upside down with one hand and gently lower the plant with the other. Roots spiralling round and round, or completely filling the compost, also indicate that a larger pot is necessary. If there are few, or no, roots visible, return the plant to its pot.

If 'potting on', as it is called, is necessary, choose a pot with a diameter 2.5 to 5 centimetres (1 to 2 inches) larger than the existing one. A much larger pot is actually harmful, as the compost not reached by the plant's roots turns sour. The new pot should be perfectly clean and, if clay, soaked for an hour before use. Crock clay pots by placing a layer of hardcore or concave shards (broken pieces of clay pots) in the bottom; plastic pots do not

An amusing one-off trick with two-and three-dimensional topiary. The shape of the plant is dictated by the shape of the graphic image.

need crocking. Place a layer of compost in the bottom of the plastic pot or over the crocking, so that the finished surface will be slightly below the rim of the pot.

Remove the plant from its old pot, and gently dislodge some of the worn-out compost clinging to the roots. Check the bottom of the root ball for any crocks caught in it, and remove any you find.

Place the root ball in the centre of the larger pot, then sift fresh compost (ideally, at room temperature) through the roots and into the space between the side of the pot and the root ball. Never switch composts 'mid-stream'; roots are reluctant to penetrate a different growing medium. Once potting on is completed firm loam-based compost; do not firm peat-based compost. Water lightly, then keep the plant out of the direct sun for a couple of days.

Sooner or later, potting on has to stop. A plant may be in the largest pot available, or the largest pot suitable for its position in the room. Or it may be infinitely slow growing, or may have stopped growing altogether, having reached its full size. In all of these cases, remove the plant from its pot every spring, tease away most of the old compost from the roots, return the plant to its pot, then replace the old compost with fresh compost. For plants too big to repot, carefully scrape away the top 2.5 centimetres (1 inch) of compost, disturbing the roots as little as possible, and replace with fresh compost.

There is a great art to growing a large plant in a small pot, involving careful feeding, watering and pruning. Growing a small plant in a large pot is pointless in terms of design, and bad horticultural practice.

Potting on

Roots growing out of the drainage hole indicate that potting on may be needed.

Thick white roots circling round the base are a further indication.

Check for caught crocks then centre in a pot one or two sizes larger.

Infill with compost, then firm if loam based, and water lightly.

DESIGNS ON PLANTS

The number of different house plants on the market is far larger than there is room for in the home. Personal taste is always the final arbiter but, like making one's way through a menu in a foreign restaurant, most people need a little experienced guidance before finally deciding.

While any well-grown plant has merit, some plants definitely have more 'dash' and presence than others: a plant's form, scale, colour or even connotations may make it stand out from the others. The following plants have been selected for their outstanding qualities or purpose.

INDOOR TREES

Indoor trees range in price from the reasonable to the extremely expensive. It is sensible to do some research and shopping around to avoid costly mistakes.

The weeping fig is a favourite indoor tree. Its evergreen, shiny leaves are graceful, yet quite ordinary in shape; that is its special charm. Indian in origin, its appearance is that of a small leaved garden tree. Frankly, the bigger a weeping fig is, the better; tiny, inexpensive, 'table-top' versions only serve as depressing reminders of the statuesque quality of the large specimens. The fiddle-leaf fig is far more exotic looking, with huge, puckered,

violin-shaped leaves. Unless its growth is pinched out, though, it tends to have the awkward, single-stemmed growth of its relative, the rubber plant. The latter deserves a mention for its sheer will to survive the most inhospitable conditions. But because it is so often consigned to the role of 'token' plant in draughty stairwells and anonymous, impersonal foyers and left to gather dust on its leaves and cigarette ends in its pot, the rubber plant is regarded as the ugly duckling of the plant world.

Almost as popular as the weeping fig are heptapleurum and the closely related brassaia. Both have leaves composed of several leaflets, arranged like the ribs of an

---

Two weeping figs, a room divider and a mirror above a fireplace play tricks with space. Low-level flowers provide changing interest and a chance for close contact. The line-up of potted plants by the fireplace forms the equivalent of a chorus line, supporting the major 'stars' of the show.

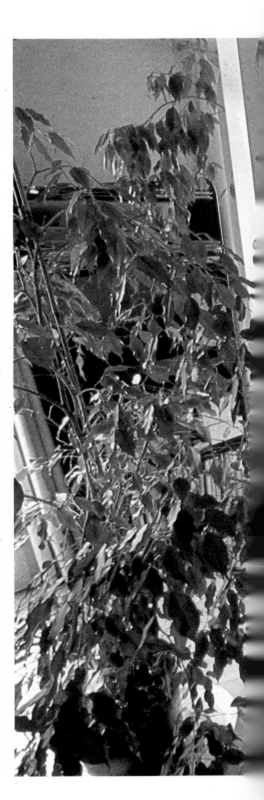

umbrella and connected to a central stalk. Like the fiddle-leaf fig and the rubber plant, heptapleurum tends to grow rocket straight unless pinched out. Brassaia – its former name was *Schefflera* and it is still often sold as this – which has larger leaves composed of fewer leaflets, is more wide-spreading in shape.

Quite different in leaf and habit of growth from all of the above is sparmannia, or African hemp. Its large leaves are pale green, heart-shaped and hairy and, in spite of its luxurious appearance, it is quite tough. Older plants do get a bit leggy, but can be cut back – the cuttings, which can be quite large, 30 centimetres (12 inches) or more in length, will root in water. In ideal conditions, sparmannia produces small white, red-centred flowers, but these are insignificant and very much a minor bonus.

Citrus trees – orange, lemon, grapefruit, kumquat – seem to have an almost irresistible appeal when in fruit: quite modest specimens carrying a single fruit sell for vast sums. The irony is that the fruit often drop off shortly afterwards, either as a result of jostling, or perhaps a sudden change of temperature, on the journey home. The plants themselves are quite attractive, with glossy, aromatic foliage and highly scented white flowers. But although they will survive in medium light levels, they will not flower, and certainly not fruit, without bright light and high summer temperatures. Seeds of citrus fruit germinate freely, but the young plants will be unknown quantities as far as flowering and fruiting performance go; cuttings are more predictable.

Dracaena marginata is ninety per cent, or more, stem: pale, slender and elegant. The single stem grows poker straight at first, and then every few years, quite unpredictably, a small bud will appear at the top of the main stem and eventually grow into a new branch, topped with a cluster of long, narrow leaves. Virtually indestructible, young plants are relatively inexpensive. *Dracaena fragrans* has much larger leaves, in length and width, and is available in several variegated forms. In time, it forms a thick-trunked tree topped by loosely clustered leaves; specimens with branches and several leaf clusters tend to be more graceful than those with a single cluster of leaves.

In its native Brazil, jacaranda grows to a huge height and has wonderful mauve

Above *Curious rather than beautiful, the pony tail, or elephant-foot plant ranges in size from table-top adornment to large-scale indoor trees. It is slow growing, and the size when bought is the size it is likely to remain.*

Right *Pollarded sparmannias, reminiscent of pollarded plane trees, make a throne-like setting for a day bed. Pairs of indoor trees can bracket a sofa, table or desk, and make using the furniture thus bracketed immensely pleasurable.*

flowers, but it is unlikely to flower or grow excessively tall as a house plant. Its foliage is downy, delicate and heavily divided, like the fronds of some ferns. It is single-stemmed when young, but when it reaches about 1 metre (3 feet) or so in height becomes attractively multi-stemmed. Traditionally, young seedlings were used as foliage 'dot' plants in mixed floral displays; specimen trees are far more impressive. However, they do need light, airy conditions and a winter rest at a temperature of about 13°C (55°F) – and so are not the easiest of indoor trees to cultivate.

Aloe arborescens, on the other hand, is extremely tolerant. It starts as a single-stemmed plant too, but quickly sends up offshoots from the base which eventually form stems of their own. Like *Dracaena marginata*, the stems become quite sinuous as they age and grow towards the light, and the effect of the stems and the loose rosettes of grey-green, succulent leaves is rather sculptural. Provided it gets enough light, *Aloe arborescens* is very long-lived, gradually increasing in size and visual value.

The Spanish bayonet tree nearly always looks awkward – its thin, even stem terminates abruptly and is surmounted by leaf rosettes which look almost as if they have been glued on. It is ironic that such an unnatural-looking plant is so popular, but perhaps it is because it's cheap, easy to propagate and almost impossible to kill.

A curiously striking rather than beautiful indoor tree is the pony tail, or elephant-foot plant. An unlikely member of the lily family, from a distance it looks like a palm with a very swollen base; its graceful evergreen leaves can be up to 1.5 metres (5 feet) long, and grow in a very pretty, fountain-like way.

INDOOR/OUTDOOR PLANTS

The plants in this category prefer summering outdoors, in a garden or on a sunny, sheltered terrace or balcony, and either need or tolerate over-wintering in a cool sun room or conservatory (see also, *Bringing the garden indoors*, pages 35–37). Many could survive the winter outdoors, if grown in the open ground in mild climates; grown in containers, their roots are more vulnerable to frosts. What these plants cannot tolerate, however, is a hot, dry winter environment.

Bay trees are a perfect example of an indoor/outdoor plant. Although you often see photographs of formally trained specimens embellishing formal sitting rooms, the bays will have been paying the briefest of visits, probably from a cool conservatory. Whether trained as a standard, pyramid or cylindrical tree, a bay is immensely attractive, and is a good, long-term investment. (Tiny sprigs of it can be removed, for use in the kitchen.)

Like bay, the myrtle is a Mediterranean evergreen shrub that can be grown outdoors in sheltered, mild conditions; unlike bay, myrtle has exquisitely scented white flowers in late summer. But unfortunately, it is not terribly attractive out of flower, as its small, aromatic pointed leaves are rather dull. To ensure flowering, you should place the plant in a sunny spot outdoors from the beginning of summer until frost threatens.

Camellias, when first imported from the Orient, were treated as tender plants. In fact, most are quite hardy, although the flowers are fragile and prone to frost damage. Young, single-stemmed plants,

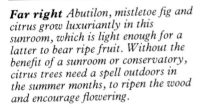

Far right *Abutilon, mistletoe fig and citrus grow luxuriantly in this sunroom, which is light enough for a latter to bear ripe fruit. Without the benefit of a sunroom or conservatory, citrus trees need a spell outdoors in the summer months, to ripen the wood and encourage flowering.*

no more than rooted cuttings, are often sold loaded down with blossom; as well as looking peculiar, this does the plant no good at all – the energy expended in the production of flowers would have been far better spent in the production of new roots, leaves and shoots. Don't buy a camellia unless it is a nicely shaped and well-proportioned plant. If a newly rooted cutting is all that you can afford, remove the flower buds, and any flowers it 'comes with' for the first two or three growing seasons.

Oleanders are also evergreen, flowering shrubs, definitely less hardy than the camellia but equally beautiful when in flower. The flowers are usually deep pink,

but can be had in other colours; double-flowered forms are heavily almond scented. The narrow, arrow-shaped leaves are rather sparse, and so is the plant's habit of growth. It is an upright plant, sometimes available trained as a standard, and any cuttings can be rooted easily in water. All parts of oleander are very poisonous.

Pittosporum is usually seen as the fore-lorn sprig of foliage tucked into a bouquet of mixed flowers. In fact, it is a handsome evergreen shrub. The one most suitable for indoor/outdoor growing is *P. tobira*. Its thick, glossy leaves are carried on slightly upright branches; the creamy-white flowers, which appear in summer,

are heavily scented like orange blossom.

Eucalyptus are interesting in that they have two types of foliage: juvenile and adult. In most cases, the juvenile foliage is more attractive and, luckily, a eucalyptus grown in a pot is unlikely to reach the adult stage of growth. There are hundreds of species; the best ones for indoor/outdoor use include *Eucalyptus gunnii*, *E. globulus* and *E. niphophila*.

Of the dozens of acacias, florists' mimosa, *Acacia dealbata*, is the easiest to come by and to grow as an indoor/outdoor plant. Its fragrant, golden-yellow, fluffy flowers are produced only if the plant's wood is ripened by hot, sunny summers. The plant is bushy, with silvery, fern-like

Above Zonal pelargoniums are as valuable indoors as they are out; given sufficient light, they are capable of flowering for weeks on end. (This specimen is ready for a bit of judicious pinching out.)

Right Though multi-colour displays of polyanthus outdoors have municipal overtones, they can be effective in the frankly artificial environment indoors. These cheap-and-cheerful, mix-and-match plants tend to look more impressive the larger the quantity used.

leaves, and can reach a considerable size if grown in a large pot.

Box elders are totally hardy and make quite big trees when grown in the open ground; if grown in pots, they remain quite small and can be brought indoors to a cool room for a short, late-winter or early-spring display. There are gold- as well as silver-variegated forms; both are more likely to be found in garden centres rather than florists' shops.

As with a standard box elder, a standard loquat would seem to be more suitably classified as an indoor tree than an indoor/outdoor plant. However, both of them should be brought indoors only for a short term in the winter months and need the rest of the year in the open air. The loquat's leaves are very large, slightly felted above and rust-brown on the undersides, and its edible orange fruit are rarely produced in temperate climates; it is easy to germinate young plants from the fruit stones.

The Australian bottle brush, which is very nearly hardy, needs exposure to summer sun to ripen its wood and encourage production of the next year's flowers. These flowers are composed of masses of bright-red stamens, tightly packed in spikes which really do resemble bottle brushes (petals are present, but are entirely hidden by the stamen). The best form for indoor/outdoor use is *Callistemon citrinus* 'Splendens'; its narrow evergreen leaves smell of lemon when crushed. The bottle brush is an unusual shrub in that the flowers are carried at the tips of branches, but the branches themselves grow on after flowering to produce more woody growth, leaves and flowers. By nature, it is a straggly shrub, so plant two or three in the same pot.

The Japanese yew, or Buddhist pine, is an unusual, glossy-leaved conifer cultivated for its foliage. Although it grows into a large tree in ideal conditions, Japanese yew remains shrubby when pot-grown. Its narrow, dark-green leaves grow in a spiral pattern around the shoot, and its habit of growth and general appearance are graceful enough not to warrant a floral display.

Indian azaleas are so often lost a month or two after flowering that they have acquired the reputation of being impossibly difficult. In fact, if they are treated as the indoor/outdoor plants that they are, chances of success will be greatly improved. Placed outdoors in a sheltered, lightly shaded spot for the summer and watered generously all year round, they should be long-lived and free-flowering.

Out-of-flower fuchsias are not very attractive, even if they retain their leaves. One eminent fuchsia breeder who had no greenhouse for over-wintering the tender cultivars solved the problem by burying the plants in a deep pit, dug each autumn before the first frost. Buried well below the frost line, the plants remained dormant until the following spring, when they were dug up, repotted and started into growth again. Although this was done of necessity, it is a true indication of just how unattractive an out-of-season fuchsia usually is.

Don't waste money on a standard fuchsia unless you have a greenhouse to protect it over the winter months, or are prepared to write it off at the end of the season.

Given sufficient light, zonal pelargoniums grown as house plants usually flower over a longer period than fuchsias. Many zonal pelargoniums have attractive leaves; so do the scented-leaved varieties.

SHORT-LIVED PLANTS

Most of the following plants are genuinely short-lived. Given ideal circumstances, a few could live for many years, but their requirements are so demanding that it would be unrealistic to try to meet them. Fortunately, many of the plants are also cheap because they are raised annually from seed, on a mass scale.

Primulas, polyanthus and primroses are for sale from early winter onwards. Their colour ranges include white and primary colours, as well as deep, rich tones and delicate pastel ones. Particularly graceful are the yellow-flowered *P. × kewensis*, and the fairy primrose.

Calceolarias and cinerarias are popular gift plants, being both colourful and cheap. The former have pouch-shaped flowers, the lower lip often spotted or edged in a contrasting colour. The latter has the typical, daisy-like flowers of the *Compositae* family to which it belongs; the flowers can be single-coloured, or ringed attractively with a second, contrasting colour. Calceolarias and cinerarias are available at much the same time as primulas, polyanthus and primrose and, like them, prefer the coolest (but frost-free) growing conditions possible.

Christmas cherry, Jerusalem cherry and ornamental pepper, or capsicum, have flowers whose only merit is that brightly coloured fruit grow from them. The leaves are very dull indeed, but the fruit should last for a month or more, given a temperature of around 10°C (50°F). Once the fruit shrivel, it is best to discard the plants.

Coleus, on the other hand, is grown for its leaves only; any tiny flower spikes that do appear are best nipped in the bud, to help keep the plant compact and bushy. Coleus is a perennial, but older plants are usually tatty and bare at the base. The best approach is to take cuttings at the end of the growing season; the cuttings root easily in water and provide the following year's display. Plant breeders have gone wild with coleus, producing intense colours and colour combinations; some are subtle, some startling and, unfortunately, some are garish and disconcerting. Choose plants with care.

Busy Lizzie operates on a similar cycle to coleus: sold small, capable of more growth and longevity than it is usually allowed, and propagated from cuttings rooted in water. Recent breeding developments have resulted in busy Lizzies with attractively variegated leaves; conventional cultivars depend for their popularity on their flowers alone.

Over the years, wax begonias have been bred into ever more compact and floriferous plants, so that many now look like explosions of pink or white; although the natural proportion of leaf to flower has been distorted, these plants still have a certain charm, especially when displayed *en masse*. Theoretically, they can be cut back by half after flowering, and taken somewhere out of view, cool and sunny to recover. In practice, most people discard them, as they tend to get leggy in the less-than-perfect light levels indoors.

Both poinsettias and chrysanthemums are raised commercially from cuttings taken annually. Both are subjected to rigorous artificial light regimes to induce them to flower when they would not otherwise do so. And both are kept artificially small by the use of dwarfing hormones. Taking cuttings from existing plants, even if successful, would result in huge specimens – up to 1.8 metres (6 feet) high – that flowered only in late autumn. Poinsettias are traditionally red, although there are pink and rather elegant white 'flowered' varieties available. In fact, the true flowers are tiny and surrounded by colourful, leaf-like bracts. Potted chrysanthemums can be had in single, semi-double and double forms, and a wide range of colours. Most refreshing are the single, daisy-like ones.

Hydrangeas are permanent fixtures in many gardens, but short-lived as house plants. Like forced bulbs, the strain of flowering ahead of their natural schedule means that they can only do it once.

Either discard them after flowering or plant out in the garden, where they will eventually recover and flower according to their normal cycle.

The poor man's orchid, or butterfly flower, is an old-fashioned favourite that was traditionally sown in summer to flower in the greenhouse or conservatory in winter. Its pink, white, purple or red flowers, all blotched with yellow, are shaped like orchids and hover above the stems like butterflies. Dwarf forms are occasionally sold in flower as pot plants; if you want the taller, 1 metre (3 feet) high plants, you will have to raise them from seed. In spite of its common name and its exotic appearance, the poor man's orchid is a member of the potato family. So, too, is another old-fashioned favourite, browallia. It will have masses of blue, star-shaped flowers up to 5 centimetres (2 inches) across all summer if sown in spring, or all winter if sown in summer. As with poor man's orchid, heights range from dwarf to quite tall; some forms are suitable for growing in hanging baskets.

The morning glory, or ipomoea, is an annual climber which can be bought, ready-grown, from garden centres. According to *Greenhouse Management for Amateurs* (1911), 'The culture of Ipomoeas is very easy and, in proportion to the beauty of the plants, may be said to be about as profitable as that of anything grown.' Quite right. Although the beautiful funnel-shaped flowers are most often blue, there are white, scarlet, crimson and purple forms; they all open early in the morning, fade later that day, and are

Left *Poinsettias symbolize the Christmas season, but this huge plant transcends such automatic symbolism, and its form and foliage are as beautiful as its creamy-white flowers.*

Below *An essay in green and white: two cyclamens, a Madagascar periwinkle, variegated ivy and creeping fig adorn a white fireplace in an all-white room.*

Above *Short-lived house plants can be used with more flamboyance and less horticultural restrictions than longer-lived, potentially permanent, plants. These hydrangeas are a case in point: beautiful while they last, disposable when they finish.*

Right *Tuberous-rooted begonias are summer pick-me-ups: cheap, cheerful and easily discarded at the end of the season. Such large-flowered hybrids are visually remote from nature, and look more at home in the artificial environment of a windowsill than in the garden proper.*

replaced with fresh blooms all through the summer months.

Madagascar periwinkle is not an annual but is treated as such because its beauty fades after the first flush of youth. The small, bushy plant carries pink, or occasionally white, star-like flowers from spring until autumn. Cuttings root easily so old plants can be an ongoing source of new ones.

Another tender perennial to be treated as a cheap and cheerful annual is cathedral bells, or cup-and-saucer vine. At the turn of the century, gardening writers advocated using it in ferneries to shade the ferns, because of its fast, large-scale and reliable summer growth. Every autumn it was cut back to allow light to penetrate the fernery – it grows up to 6 metres (20 feet) annually – and the following spring the new growth was trained up to the ceiling. Today, it is grown annually from seed, mainly for its large, purple, bell-shaped flowers and unusual lovely green, saucer-shaped calyces.

SEASONAL SPLENDOUR

Some plants disappear completely for part or most of the year. Those with greenhouses can consign the dormant plants to exile there; those without can either discard the plant when its first display is over, or live with it until it starts into growth the following year.

Cyclamen is a prime example. If you can keep it rested or active, as appropriate, you will be rewarded with up to forty or fifty blossoms over a period of three months or more. The secrets of success are: keeping the plant cool; providing a humid environment; watering from be-

low, and gradually drying the corm off when flowering is over. You should keep the corm bone dry during the summer months, then repot it in fresh compost and give it slowly increasing amounts of water, reversing the drying off process.

Tuberous-rooted begonias are summer-flowering equivalents. Their huge, waxy, almost plastic, flowers seem unreal in their symmetry, perfection and size. Given the same treatment as cyclamen, but the tubers dried off when the leaves begin to yellow in autumn and started off into growth in early spring, these begonias can last for many summers.

Hippeastrum, or amaryllis as it is sometimes called, has a peculiar cycle all of its own: dormancy is broken by the production of an erect, and rather ungainly, flower stalk, which in turn produces lavish, rich-looking, trumpet-shaped flowers; these are followed by the arching, strap-shaped leaves which remain until summer, when they, too, disappear. Still, it is worth noting that a newly bought hippeastrum will be in flower for one month of the year. Older hippeastrums are not dependable, and often concentrate their energy on leaf production instead of blooms.

While tuberous-rooted begonias and hippeastrums are often sold in their dormant state (pre-packaged in boxes which use images of the fully-grown flowers as a lure), caladium, or angel's wings, are sold only when in leaf. Colour and interest are provided by the huge, paper-thin leaves, which are present in spring and summer, and absent the rest of the year. Unlike cyclamen, tuberous-rooted begonia and hippeastrum, caladium is very temperamental, requiring high heat and humidity and a total absence of draughts. Only the

devoted are likely to get repeat action out of this plant.

The pretty little *Campanula isopylla*, so often seen overspilling pots and hanging baskets with masses of starry blue or white flowers, is an almost hardy perennial. Although needing frost-free conditions, it behaves like herbaceous perennials in the garden: dying back at the end of the growing season and reappearing in spring. If it doesn't rest for several months in cool conditions, it simply won't flower.

Another summer-flowering trailing plant is achimines, or the hot water plant. The flowers, which are short-lived but produced in great profusion, can be pink, blue, violet, white, salmon or bi-coloured, with contrasting markings on the 'throats'. The rhizomes, which produce the plants, need total rest for a good six months of the year.

Forced bulbs – hyacinths, tulips, daffodils and crocus – fall half-way between the 'Repeat action' and 'Short-lived' plant categories. Bulbs that have been specially treated to flower at Christmas-time, well in advance of their outdoor counterparts, and untreated bulbs that have been forced in very warm conditions, will be worn out at the end of flowering. These plants cannot be forced again; once their flowers have faded they should either be planted out in the garden, where they will eventually recover and flower at the normal time, or be discarded. Bulbs that have been forced very gently in cool conditions – a slightly heated sun room, for example – can be used for display year after year; the gentler the forcing, the less stressful for the plant. Still, the plants must be returned to the garden after flowering – ideally to the sheltered environment of a cold frame – then fed, watered and rested until the following late winter or early spring when they start over again.

There are many lesser known tender bulbs, corms and tubers which are also worth pursuing. The glory lily is a deciduous, tuberous-rooted climber with flowers of exquisite design and detail. The brilliant red, yellow-edged blooms, carried at the tips of the stems in summer, are like wavy-edged Turk's cap lilies. The image of the glory lily's flower, in bulb catalogues or on packages containing the dormant tuber, is irresistible. But this tropical African plant is not easy to grow from its dormant state, since it requires heat, high humidity and exact watering and feeding regimes.

South African bulbous plants often die down completely for part of the year in response to the seasonal heat and drought of their native environment. One example is the blood lily, with its showy bracts surrounding bright red stamens. Others include the Scarborough lily, which is similar in appearance to a red-flowered hippeastrum; veltheimia, with tiny, tubular pink flowers, and lachenalias, with tubular flowers ranging in colour from yellow, through orange, red and purple to green and sometimes multi-colours.

Ginger lilies, also known as garland flowers or butterfly lilies, are deliciously scented tender perennials, with flowers that look like honeysuckle and leafy growth similar to old-fashioned canna lilies. Their flowers are mostly lemon and orange, but some specialist nurseries can supply pink, white, red and cream ones. The flower stems, which can be up to 1.5 metres (5 feet) high, need to be cut down once the flowers fade. Non-flowering shoots, produced in late summer, can be left on the plant, to flower the next spring.

Above *The rigid growth of the hippeastrum is fascinating to watch. Such plants can be bought, 'ready-made', in flower, but as well as the risk of getting them home in one piece, the pleasure of anticipation is gone.*

Left *Botanical prints and forced tulips in a range of warm colours and immaculately simple containers shape this collection, which is controlled without feeling contrived.*

ARCHITECTURAL PLANTS

There is a whole group of plants which can be called 'architectural': they include plants beloved by architects, plants with architectural qualities and, paradoxically, plants whose feathery foliage is used as a contrast to the severity of modern architectural form. Overall, it is a group of plants that displays form and foliage rather than flowers.

Monsteras, philodendrons and rubber plants were often featured in early illustrations of modern architecture, because of their large, simple leaves. Scale, as much as form, was an important consideration, and still is. For this reason, indoor trees (see pages 68–73) are favourites; trees are large enough to make an impact on an interior, and to act as a focal point, not as clutter.

Architects and interior designers have long had a working partnership with palms. In fact, any palms that do manage to survive outdoors in temperate climates often look bedraggled; indoors, they fare better, especially in homes without central heating. In winter central heating is the main enemy of the European fan palm, Chinese fan palm, date palm, lady palm, windmill palm and desert fan palm. Other species – the fishtail palm, coconut palm, parlour palm, kentia palm and yellow palm – are more tolerant, but all these plants benefit from a humid atmosphere in warm temperatures. Although palms need bright light to flourish, lack of direct sunlight is not a problem. In nature, the young plants grow in the shade of nearby plants; small palms are generally young and need protection from direct light.

Architectural plants include those of simple form and large scale. Such plants as these – philodendron, yucca and weeping fig – add to the pleasure of being in a room without competing with other features or hindering daily activities.

The natural structure of desert cacti and succulents is intriguing, but the plants have to be quite large to make an impact; because they are slow-growing, large specimens are expensive. Another catch is that both desert cacti and succulents are very demanding in terms of light requirements and extremely vulnerable to over-watering.

At the other end of the light scale, and equally 'architectural', are the ferns. Like palms, most ferns thrive in cool rooms that are not centrally heated. Like cacti, the larger ferns are, the more impact they make. Most dramatic, and perhaps atypical, is the stag's horn fern, an epiphyte from the temperate regions of Australia. It is sculptural rather than pretty, and mature specimens need plenty of space. Another superb epiphyte is the bird's nest fern; being tropical in origin, it needs humid and warmer conditions. Its fronds are arranged in a shuttlecock formation and can grow to 1 metre (3 feet) in length, although it rarely does in cultivation.

The Boston fern, or sword fern, was obligatory in every Victorian home. Large specimens are best displayed on pedestals or in hanging baskets, from which the lower fronds can arch and droop gracefully. A fern that could be classified as both 'Architectural' and 'Short-lived' is the maidenhair. It is exquisite in its form and delicacy, but difficult to keep happy outside the confines of a humid terrarium.

Although botanically closer to lilies than to ferns, asparagus 'ferns' are amenable and popular house plants. *Asparagus sprengeri* is the one most often seen; it can grow to a huge size and occasionally surprises its owner (and reveals its botanical connections) by producing small red berries. More temperamental, and visu-

ally more delicate, is *A. plumosus*, the florists' asparagus fern. Use it in a supporting role, allowing it to weave through other plants.

Two that are difficult to find but worth pursuing are the foxtail fern, *Asparagus densiflorus* 'Myers' or *A. myersii*, and the sicklethorn, *A. falcatus*. The foxtail fern looks like its common name suggests; several massive green plumes arching rather than trailing in form. Even more erect is sicklethorn, which can reach 3m (10 ft) in height and benefits from a bit of support if there is insufficient space for it to arch and spread out naturally.

Plants forming rosettes, with leaves growing concentrically from a central point, have a natural symmetry and appeal, although some rosettes are looser, and slightly more haphazard, than others. Most bromeliads are rosette formers, and include the urn plant, ornamental pineapple, queen's tears, guzmania, tillandsia, flaming sword and blushing bromeliads. Large specimens always look good, especially when displayed below eye-level. Generally, these plants need bright light, warmth, relatively small pots, little food, and the central cup formed by the rosette kept full of water. Agaves are non-bromeliad rosette formers and need less water and more direct sunlight.

Far left *These four coconut palms make a design statement larger than the sum of its parts.*

Left *The stag's horn fern is intriguingly sculptural and large-scale specimens, such as this one, are automatic focal points.*

Plants with strongly vertical growth, such as aspidistra, mother-in-law's tongue and umbrella, have a strong architectural presence. Aspidistra and mother-in-law's tongue, like the rubber plant, are often chosen as 'token' plants and left to collect dust in some corner, and their reputation has suffered rather unfairly.

CLIMBING AND HANGING PLANTS

Vertical space is valuable for plants, especially if you have very little floor space. Provided they are sited out of the normal traffic route yet are easy enough to reach for routine maintenance, hanging and climbing plants can soften and even define interior space without cluttering it. Plants of naturally arching or loose habit can be grown in hanging baskets. So, too, can epiphytes, which grow in nature on the branches and trunks of forest trees; many bromeliads and orchids are epiphytic, as are some ferns. Trailing plants can also be grown in hanging baskets, although those that are quick-growing or become very big are perhaps better trained up canes, wires or trellis work.

The all-time favourites among hanging-basket plants have achieved their popularity because they tolerate a certain amount of neglect and a range of growing conditions. Chief among these is the spider plant, followed by the various asparagus ferns. The latter are attractive and tough in equal measure; emerald fern is the form most usually seen, but the foxtail fern is equally pretty. The asparagus fern used as cut foliage by florists (usually half-heartedly) can also be grown in hanging baskets, although the plants

Above *Asparagus ferns are popular, and justifiably so. They have easy-going temperaments, come in several sizes and shapes – all of which are pretty – and are widely available.*

Right *A high-level curtain of philodendron, with a few trailing stems of passion flower, confuse the boundary between indoors and out, in the nicest possible way. On a practical level, the plants are higher than head height, and any wayward growth can easily be tied up or snipped off.*

Above *A curtain of philodendron again, in the more formal setting of a sitting room. Plants help soften and humanize the severity of modern architectural designs, though maintaining the balance between the two is important.*

Right *A variegated piggy-back plant rises to the occasion of an immaculate setting and sculptural stand. This humble, 'mother-and-baby' plant is equally at home in a hanging basket and informal surroundings, and is hardy enough to be grown as ground cover in sheltered gardens.*

eventually send out quite long climbing stems. Wandering Jew (*Tradescantia* and *Zebrina*) is often seen in hanging baskets, either as the sole occupant or as part of mixed planting. Because it is quick-growing, wandering Jew does tend to get sparse and leggy at the base and needs regular pinching out of the tips.

More adventurous plants for hanging baskets include the creeping fig and the graceful bulrush. Both, though, need very careful watering; the creeping fig must never be allowed to dry out, while the bulrush must be kept continually moist as long as the temperature is above 13°C (55°F) and nearly dry if the temperature falls lower.

Various 'mother and baby' plants are excellent in hanging baskets. As well as the spider plant, the two plants commonly called mother of thousands, *Saxifraga* and *Tolmeia*, are ideal; the former dangles its 'babies' at the tips of stolons, or runners, while the latter produces them on the upper surfaces of the leaves, at the junction of leaf and leaf stalk. Likewise, the dainty hen-and-chicken fern, which produces its young on the upper surfaces of its fronds. All three plants are very nearly hardy, and need cool winter temperatures.

Hearts entangled is a sun-loving tuberous-rooted trailer which produces tiny tubers rather than fully developed plantlets along the length of its trailing stems. Another sun-loving, hanging-basket plant with an unlikely reproduction method is the succulent sedum, donkey's tail. Its fleshy, greyish green leaves are easily dislodged from the trailing stems; should the leaves fall on to a suitable compost, they will send out roots.

The miniature wax plant is more suitable for hanging baskets than its rampant relative, the ordinary hoya. The latter looks more natural trained upwards, tied to trellis work or wires, than around a wire circle. The same applies to stephanotis and jasmine. Of these three scented flowering climbers, stephanotis is the most temperamental, requiring higher temperatures, more humidity and less temperature fluctuation than either hoya or jasmine. It also needs protection from direct sunlight, whereas jasmine and hoya both flower better with some exposure to full sun.

Bougainvillea, passionflower and Cape leadwort seem unlikely bedfellows, but they share many of the same visual strengths and weaknesses. All have beautiful flowers and a mesmerizing presence when well grown. On the minus side, their leaves are rather dull, and their habits of growth not particularly attractive. As all three need exposure to direct sunlight to flower well, coupled with a cool winter rest period, they are often disappointing house plants after their first flush of flowering. Still, in a conservatory or sun room with more amenable conditions, any of them could make a spectacular contribution to the scene.

Non-flowering, but more dependable, climbers include ivy in all its forms, grape ivy, kangaroo vine, devil's ivy, heartleaf philodendron, and variegated peperomia. Certainly they lack the 'glitzy' presence of more exotic plants, but they do perform admirably in less than perfect growing conditions.

Half-way between climbers and self-supporting plants are *Fatshedera* (a cross between ivy and fatsia), monstera and various philodendrons – again, non-flowering but tolerant and useful. *Fatshedera* has not inherited ivy's ability to

send out aerial roots, and needs to be permanently tied to its support. Monstera and philodendron produce aerial roots which can be trained to cling to moss poles, although the plants can be supported conventionally.

None of the following is an easy plant to find or to grow in a hot, dry, centrally heated house. They are all attractive, though, and worth trying if you have a cool, bright sun room or conservatory.

The Chilean bellflower, or Napoleon's bell, is a large evergreen climber with twining shoots, heart-shaped leaves and exquisitely beautiful bell-shaped flowers. These flowers are fleshy, usually deep crimson, and hang in clusters in summer and autumn; they last for a month or more when cut. Glory pea, parrot's bill and lobster claw are all common names for the same scandent shrub, *Clianthus puniceus*. A member of the pea family, it has attractive, pinnate leaves and claw-like bright crimson flowers appear in early summer. Unless tied firmly to trellis work or wires, glory pea will behave in the same way as winter-flowering jasmine, forming a sloppy mound at ground level. Both the Chilean bellflower and glory pea have rare, white-flowered forms. In both cases, the white flowers are more subtle, perhaps even more tasteful, than the vivid pink of the species, but some of their exotic beauty is lost in the exchange.

Chinese jasmine and Chilean jasmine both have heavily fragrant white flowers. Confusingly, neither is remotely related to jasmine – a common problem with common names. They are actually members of the periwinkle family, with typical, star-like, periwinkle flowers. Chinese jasmine is evergreen, which makes it a better choice than the deciduous Chilean jasmine.

USING FLOWERS

Flowers have for so long been automatic symbols of hospitality that their presence at social events is taken for granted. Flower arranging, likewise, has become so ritualized that the inherent beauty of a flower is often lost in clichéed formality. Rediscover the potential of flowers, whether bought or home grown, wildly expensive or free.

Cut flowers should always enhance, never intimidate or bore. A bunch of mixed flowers picked straight from the garden and displayed with a minimum of adjustment or arrangement brings a homely, relaxing touch to a room. Those without a garden need not despair: a dozen daffodils bought from a local stall or shop, and displayed in a simple glass jug, has the same unpretentious informality of a garden bouquet. A bunch of violets or snowdrops is far more enjoyable than a formal arrangement of florists' flowers costing many times as much. In any case, large-scale formal arrangements are usually pompous and sometimes meant simply as conspicuous displays of wealth; smaller formal arrangements lose some of their pomposity, but still manage to remain remote from nature and the viewer.

PERFECT CHOICES

Some flowers are almost impossible to misuse, whether displayed as a single stem or bunch. Although traditionally confined to the role of filler, sprays of baby's breath make a delicate white cloud, their tiny individual blooms successfully disproving the 'big is automatically beautiful' theory.

Arum lilies are another sure-fire success. They are inherently beautiful, and were once a symbol of the art nouveau movement; the flowers are as appropriate in contemporary interiors as they are in those with a period flavour. Anthurium flowers, with their white, pink, salmon or red sail-like spathe and long central spikes, look bizarre and highly unconventional – and quite beautiful.

There are no inelegant lilies; breeders have not yet burdened them with huge size or crude coloration (Turk's cap lilies, though, have a distinctly foxy smell, which many people find unpleasant). Use a single stem or a generous bunch of lilies – some in bud, some partly open, others fully open. Certain lilies are sold by the stem and are very expensive. The cost of a dozen stems might easily equal that of a large formal arrangement, but the lilies present their own quiet beauty first.

Using multiples of a single flower is

Cut flowers, like house plants, should be both welcoming and a complement to the mood and style of an interior.

always visually effective. One, two, three or even four dozen red tulips in an all-white room have a very strong presence that is far stronger than a mixed bunch of florist's flowers.

Seasonal references are always welcome, whether they are one jump ahead of nature or mirror exactly what is going on in the garden. Large branches of flowering quince, forsythia, flowering currant, viburnum, lilac or deutzia, cut from the shrub when the flower buds are showing, can be forced gently indoors. The branches need no accompaniment other than a very simple and stable container. Displayed against a pale wall, they take on an architectural quality – simple and magnificent. Fruit tree prunings can receive a second life indoors, to provide delicate blossom for weeks on end. As with forcing trees and shrubs indoors, make sure fat flower buds are visible, or you may end up with new leaves and no flowers.

Home-grown flowers, like home-made bread, have special value because they are a unique reflection of your taste and are absolutely fresh. The choice from any one garden may be more limited than the standardized fare offered by florists, but the flowers provide scope for a more personal, and therefore memorable, display.

Right *White tulips, button chrysanthemums and variegated ivy make their home under, not on, a glass-topped table.*

Far right *Asters and Japanese anemones cut florists' gladioli down to size, and the hugely exuberant informality of the former counteracts the natural rigidity of the latter.*

The foliage available from a reasonable-sized garden – even leafless branches full of rose-hips, crab apple or spindle berry – is invaluable and should be used generously and informally. The best displays of cut garden flowers are varied and changed in response to what is in season. The first rose-bud of early summer might nestle in a bouquet of forget-me-nots, sweet Williams and stars-of-Bethlehem. In high summer, jugs, vases and bowls could be overspilling with roses alone. The last remaining rose of November might share a small glass with a few sprigs of holly in berry and a stem of paper-thin honesty seed pods. Instead of six of everything, a bunch of garden flowers can contain two dozen of one flower, one or two of another and three or four of something else. The next week, reverse the proportions.

Today, some adventurous florists are augmenting their supply of commercially grown flowers with garden flowers and foliage supplied by private growers. A simple posy of cottage-garden flowers and hosta leaves might cost the earth, but it is money well spent.

Wild flowers, even weeds, can be as visually seductive as cultivated flowers. They are a very effective foil to the more thoroughbred blooms; the staid, perfectly machined appearance of long-stemmed roses can be made more homely and cheerful surrounded with ripe ears of wild barley; the predictability of double chrysanthemums can be relieved by branches of wild blackberry, in flower or fruit. Do approach picking wild flowers and weeds with care. Get permission from the owner of the land before you take any plant material; in addition, many plants are protected by law and it is illegal to gather seed, dig them up or pick them.

Left A happy marriage of natural form and High-Tech setting. Hosta leaves – far more beautiful than hosta flowers – and ornamental alliums need no apology or extra help in this bold interior. There is no floral nostalgia here, but then none is required.

Above Huge, sculptural sprays of forsythia, winter-flowering almond and laurel are paired with yellow tulips – foraging in the garden combined with a trip to the florist. The result is a statement about spring, simple, direct and as warming as the glow of the nearby fire.

PROBLEMS

The biggest floral problem is combating the ubiquitous formal bunch of florists' flowers: the chrysanthemums, carnations, iris, roses and gladioli it always seems to contain are available month in, month out, in standard sizes, shapes and colours, as if manufactured rather than grown. That said, it is far better to have flowers than no flowers at all, and there are solutions to most floral problems. The most obvious one is to dismantle a formal flower arrangement, using as many vases as there are types of flowers if need be.

A tall, straight-sided glass vase holding two or three stems of white gladioli extracted from a mixed bunch can be very elegant. Or you can dilute the potential anonymity of gladioli by giving them unexpected company: branches of thorn in berry, or pine or larch, or masses of autumnal bracken. Any of the flowers in a mixed bunch can be rescued and treated in the same way: simply presented on their own or as part of a refreshing and casual composite display. In winter, try white chrysanthemums, carnations or roses with red-barked dogwood or purple-barked willow; dark-green holly spiked with red carnations or red roses; chrysanthemums in autumnal tones in similarly coloured beech and smoke-tree foliage.

If you have access to florists' foliage only, buy eucalyptus or pittosporum in large quantities. Both are expensive but long lasting and can be used again and again. With a single sprig of foliage you are very limited; it can be treated like a single red rose – alone in a tall, narrow vase – or be lost and ineffective as the token greenery in a mixed bunch.

Lack of money should not be an excuse for lack of flowers. Large supermarkets often sell nasturtium flowers in their fresh vegetable department. The intensely yellow orange and scarlet flowers are meant to be used as a garnish, but they look exquisite floating in a clear glass bowl. For the cost of a lettuce you have a marvellous dining-table centrepiece. Bright-green, ferny carrot foliage can be had for free. So, too, can prunings from your own house plants. Quick-growing wandering Jew or begonias that have grown bare at the base should be cut back for their own good and the cuttings incorporated in a bunch of flowers. (Many of the prunings will form roots in the water, and can be potted up after the show.) The umbrella plant grows as happily in pure water as it does in compost: invest in one, keep it in a wide-necked, waterproof container, and use its lovely foliage as the setting for a changing display of cut flowers.

DRIED FLOWERS

Although technically corpses, dried flowers retain much of the delicacy and attraction that they had in life. While, theoretically, dried flowers have the ability to go on for ever, they do go mouldy in damp conditions and fade in strong sunlight. They are also fragile, so must be treated with care.

Dried flowers are softer in colour than fresh and artificial ones. Green usually turns to tones of grey, beige, silver, russet or brown, and with occasional exceptions – bright yellow yarrow, for instance – the blossom is evenly low key. Consequently, a bunch of dried flowers often has a visual coherence that would be lacking if those

Far left *Morning glories are the stars of this admittedly short-lived but glorious show. Stocks, spider chrysanthemums, arctotis, acanthus and garden foliage are combined without regard to convention or provenance, with staggeringly beautiful results.*

Above *Winter prunings, normally consigned to the bonfire or dustbin, form the basis of this extraordinary display. Delicate florist's ranunculus are given substance, and appear even more fragile when seen against the rough woody growth. Viburnum berries make a fleeting reference to the winter garden, and florist's euphorbia plays a cameo role.*

Left *Never rule out house plants as a source of unusual foliage for cut flowers. Here, the umbrella-like leaves of cyperus combine with de Caen anemones, florist's foliage and puffy green thorn apple seed pods in a suitably stark display for a modern setting.*

same flowers were displayed in their fresh state. Dried flowers are automatically empathetic to any interior based on natural materials and neutral colours.

Dyeing fresh flowers is no longer in vogue but dried flora is dyed sometimes. The colours, ranging from pastel to virulent, can be attractive, but the more intense the dyes, the less natural looking, especially when the dye penetrates flowers and stems alike. On the other hand, the intensely naturalistic colours retained by drying flora in sand, silica gel or borax are paid for in other ways; flora thus mummified is vulnerable to the smallest amount of atmospheric moisture, and is usually displayed in airtight glass or plastic domes, recalling specimens in museums. The best choice is 'open air' dried flowers, which seem more life-like.

Dried flowers usually have poker-straight stems, from being dried upside down. Foliage pressed flat under heavy weights is also graceless, although glycerined material tends to retain its natural shape. You can treat poker-straight dried material as three-dimensional geometry, creating right-angled structures in blocks of colour, of one or more levels. A ziggurat of dried flowers has no pretence of being natural, but can have great beauty. Dried

Dried flowers far beyond the traditional, fiercely yellow yarrow and dusty purple and pink statice. Treat dried flowers with the imagination and sense of adventure they deserve.

flower heads can be attached to wire stems, which can be made to arch gracefully, but which also need camouflaging with infill material. Or use dried grasses and glycerined material with a naturally arching habit to mask straight stems. Least successful is the semi-explosion effect of straight stems, evenly spaced, radiating from a central point.

Dried flowers, like fresh ones, are often sold in uninspired pre-mixed combinations: mixed colours of statice and straw flowers; Chinese lanterns, yarrow, pampas grass and bulrushes, for instance. The garden, the countryside or even a local patch of waste ground offer less obvious material for drying – dock, sorrel, teasel and foxglove seed heads, or wild clematis seed heads. Collect winter branches of alder, hazel or larch, with their lovely catkins and cones, to add weight and interest to a bunch of dried flowers. Or use the branches as the basis for a dried flower 'tree', which can be either conical or round, and large or small.

Because they are naturally iightweight, if you display dried flowers in an equally lightweight container – wickerwork, woven wood or bamboo for example – put it well out of harm's way. If the container is opaque, you can fill it with marbles or other ballast, for stability.

Often discarded or put away at the first sign of cheap daffodils in the shops, dried flowers are, in fact, valid as permanent features, although they often suffer neglect because of this permanence. From time to time, check for broken stems, missing flower heads, or gaps in the display (especially if there are children around). And don't forget to dust them. Try to rearrange the display occasionally, refreshing it with new material.

A double and very witty trompe l'oeil. *Fake perspective and fake hydrangeas together make a totally real impact. Artificial flowers used in a cowardly or formal way inevitably fail. Used with flair, even outrageous flair, they can overcome their limitations and factory origins.*

Coming up tulips

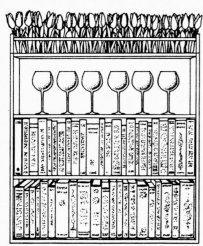

Some artificial tulips are so outrageously believable that they deserve large-scale, centre-stage treatment. Here a dowel keeps a field of fake tulips blooming endlessly in position on top of a bookcase. The tighter the flowers are packed together, the more effective the display.

Large bowls of pot-pourri can enliven a room with scent as well as muted colour. Try layering several colours of pot-pourri in a glass bowl. The flowers that provide the petals lose their individuality, but the resulting mixture, with its old-fashioned connotations, is attractive on its own.

FAKE FLOWERS

In America many years ago, a manufacturer gave away long-stemmed red plastic roses with packets of detergent. Each rose was identical, the red unrelieved by any variation in colour or thickness, the stems exactly the same length with the same number and distribution of plastic thorns – there were two, identical, snap-on leaves per rose. Fake flowers have come a long way since this humble, if not humiliating, exercise.

Because artificial flowers are meant to be used (usually) as stand-ins for real ones, guidelines that apply to using fresh flowers often apply to fake ones as well. The traditional formal arrangements are still lethal and equally static and unimaginative are the L-shaped, triangular pyramidal and curved arrangements.

A direct, informal approach suits real flowers but is vital for artificial ones. A huge woven basket filled with branches of fake forsythia in flower; a dozen artificial tulips, iris or daffodil in a glass vase or jug; a glass tank of tall spikes of artificial delphiniums is refreshingly simple. The forsythia or delphiniums could also be displayed at floor level.

Mixed artificial flowers are more difficult to get right. Conventional mixtures can be boring. Unlikely combinations – Christmas roses and lilac, for example –

might startle the seasoned gardener and upset the purist. Still, certain *nouvelle cuisine* combinations – duck breast and raspberry purée – and interior design combinations – modern tubular chairs and antique Persian carpets – are equally surprising. It just has to look right.

Although artificial stems are stronger than natural ones, they are the weakest part of the flower visually, and while the detail of individual blossoms is faithfully copied, no attempt is made to capture the difference in the colours and textures between various stems. You could decapitate dozens of artificial flowers and fill a huge glass bowl with just the blossoms, layered like a rainbow or in stripes according to the colour of the room. Or fill a garden trug, on a table, with 'freshly cut flowers'. Their stems need not be visible and you could change the flowers from time to time to 'match' the seasons.

Artificial flowers with plastic or waterproofed wire stems can be used in conjunction with real foliage: fake peonies and real holly; fake lupins massed with real eucalyptus; fake orange tiger lilies and real golden-leaved philadelphus; fake daisies and masses of real pittosporum; deep-brown fake chrysanthemums with branches of silver-leaved Moroccan broom; fake pale lilac and copper beech. Keep the combination simple and the proportions generous. If the artificial flowers have absorbent stems they can be used with artificial foliage, though artificial foliage is always obvious. Preserved foliage would be better: fake orange dahlias and dried bracken; fake pale-blue hyacinths and preserved mahonia; fake African lilies and preserved evergreen magnolia leaves; branches of fake cherry and masses of dried grasses.

Don't be afraid to be outrageous with fake flora; after all, it calls for an unconventional response. The top shelf of a bookcase could hold a thickly packed 'field' of tulips. Let fake ivy creep along a picture rail; the thicker the vegetation the better. Make a frieze of fake mimosa over the door in a garden room or over the mirror in a dark, grim bathroom. Hang small posies of artificial violets from kitchen shelving.

SETTINGS

Some interiors have a definite style or period flavour and there are flowers to match the moods: a cottage-garden posy for a country farmhouse, long-petalled spider chrysanthemums for an oriental-style bedroom and a stark bunch of steel-blue sea holly in a modern room. Such combinations can't be faulted. But it is also exciting to contrast flowers with their surroundings. Flowers can be used for emphasis or for contrast, but always use them with conviction.

The more clear open space around a floral display, the more drama is created. However, flowers can also be successful as bit players in a non-floral display: a collection of old jugs can be brought to life by filling one or two of them with fresh flowers. Floor-level floral displays automatically attract attention; make sure they are stable, large enough to be seen, and sited out of harm's way. A floral centrepiece on a dining-room table is almost obligatory but a generous bunch of tulips by the side of a bathroom sink or next to the bath itself demands as much attention. Place a container of flowers to one side of the table, rather than dead in the centre.

Far left Anthurium flowers and leaves are striking rather than pretty, a description which applies equally to this thirties-style room.

Left Vases need be packed full of flowers to fulfil their purpose. Here, container and contents work in unison to attract the eye and admiration.

Whether it is better to have one large display in the living room or several smaller displays throughout the house is a matter of personal taste and budget.

CONTAINERS

Simple containers allow the flowers to perform without competition. The least competitive containers of all are clear glass. Provided both are clean, they and the water they hold do little more than cast shadows and reflect light. There are badly designed glass containers as well as beautiful ones, however; those based on plain geometric shapes are inherently restful and attractive. Simple glazed pottery containers, in colours matching or contrasting in with the flowers, are usually equally good.

More personal, even eccentric, choices of container, gleaned from junk or antique shops, kitchen supply stores or the kitchen itself, should not be dismissed out of hand. Terracotta flower pots, with water-filled jars concealed inside, can hold cut flowers as well as rooted plants, and the two sorts together would make an amusing display. An extravagant antique container can give modest flowers a sense of grandeur; wild grasses tumbling out of a hand-painted porcelain vase, or daisies in a Georgian silver teapot, are just two examples. Try giving posh flowers a modest container: a plain glass vase brimming with rare orchids, or, on a larger scale, bird-of-paradise flowers with a salt-glazed bread crock for a vase.

Left These bright-yellow coreopsis are contained, not arranged, and their informality echoes the mood and style of their country-cottage home.

THE VIEW OUT

The view from a window is as much a part of the interior as a painting or print on the wall. While you may have little or no control of the vista, using plants creatively, on both sides of the window pane, is a real option. They can hide a multitude of eyesores and make a delightful view even more so.

Paved entrance areas form a visual extension of a house's interior and should intimate pleasures to come: clipped bays in Versailles tubs standing sentry near a front door indicate one attitude to life; honeysuckle, informal and slightly dishevelled, growing in a halved wooden barrel, indicates another. Whatever plants you choose, remember they should be upright and well behaved near a door. Uncontrollable sprawlers, heavily thorned or unpleasantly scented plants are unsuitable. And visually the space near a door is too precious, whatever the size of the garden, to waste on uninteresting plants.

Traditionally, rosemary bushes outside the front door ensure that the occupants never lack friends. Rosemary has two more advantages: it releases a pleasant, long-lasting aroma if touched and, being evergreen, provides year-round coverage. Other evergreen plants for sun or light shade and for pots or the open ground include Irish yew, camellia, box, *Fatsia japonica* and its curious offspring, *Fatshedera × lizei*. Large pots of bamboo make unusual and suitably vertical focal points; don't let their roots dry out, and provide shade from strong summer sun.

New Zealand flax is technically an evergreen perennial, but its huge, sword-like leaves give it a shrubby stature.

A containerized tree next to a door can never grow too big nor will its roots harm the building's foundations – and its presence can make even the most anonymous entrance charming. Fig trees have long been associated with domesticity; when their roots are confined in pots, their rampant growth is controlled. Although figs are not evergreen and lack conventional flowers, their pale, spreading architectural form, their huge lobed leaves and the shadows they cast make up for it. *Cordyline australis* has a poker-straight stem topped with narrow, evergreen leaves; like the fig, it needs sun and shelter. Unfortunately, both trees are usually sold as quite small plants. For those with less patience, there are many trees available 'off the peg' as 1.8 metre (6 feet) high standards. The silver weeping pear, winter-flowering cherry, golden-leaved gleditsia and ornamental crab apple are pretty choices. Plant the trees in large tubs, and underplant with spring bulbs and biennials, summer bedding plants, and winter-flowering bulbs.

Above *A camellia in a traditional white-painted Versailles tub. Camellias in full flower can be immensely seductive, so much so that people often turn a blind eye to the shape of the plant itself. This slightly gawky specimen barely earns its keep out of season, but does put on an extravagant, if brief, display, to make up for it.*

Left *Paved entrance areas form a visual extension to the house and, for the visitor, should intimate a sense of the style within. Lack of open ground is never an excuse for lack of greenery. In this brick-surfaced forecourt, standard privets (Ligustrum delavayanum) and ball-clipped boxes enliven an otherwise sparse setting. Over-elaborate flower pots, or plastic ones, would have detracted from the scene.*

WINDOW DRESSING

The closer a plant is to a window, the more impact it has on the view out or in. If you are next to a window, hyacinths on the sill or in a window box seem much larger, and somehow more real, than a huge tree away in the distance.

Plants may be used, inside or outside a window, to obscure an ugly view, but they also reduce the amount of light coming in. Masses of gold privet makes an enchanting compromise: grown against a window, it reduces the light but gives the light that does enter the room a lovely glow. And by obscuring a deadly dull view, it also gives the imagination full rein over the landscape beyond. Jugs full of cut branches of golden privet on a windowsill have a similar effect.

Huge plate-glass windows overlooking an uninterrupted landscape are thought to make a room seem larger. But an uninterrupted large-scale view, no matter how dramatic, can have the unreality of a picture postcard and a dwarfing effect on the interior and people within. The famous Glass House built by the American architect Philip Johnson is actually surrounded by trees, whose trunks act as visual walls

Right *In contemporary, glass-walled houses the view out becomes the visual enclosure. Generally, planting near the glass, as here, is extremely successful.*

Far right *Garden plants, such as the Virginia creeper illustrated, can provide the walls and curtains of an indoor-outdoor room, filtering the light and creating an 'enclosure'.*

to provide a sense of enclosure. Whether outside in the garden or indoors in pots, substantial plants next to the window will make the view more believable and more human in scale. And, as you move around the room, the relationship of the plants to the landscape beyond constantly changes in a variety of different, interesting ways.

Whatever the size of the window, it is always pleasant to have a glimpse, from inside, of permanent plants growing on the outside wall of the house. While plants should never make a window impossible to open, or undermine the structure of the building, a gentle overlap of greenery softens the view out and gives a sense of season. In autumn, the hanging stems of Boston ivy or Virginia creeper are covered in brilliant foliage that can tint the light entering a room a warm red. Looking out through a window edged with species clematis in spring; clematis hybrids, roses or wisteria in summer; and ivy or winter-flowering jasmine in winter, more than compensates for a partial loss of light. If, and when, the plants become too invasive, simply prune the excess growth and use it, in jugs or vases, to decorate the room. There is no more direct way to bring the outdoors in.

CONTAINERS

Always buy the largest pot you have the space for. A large pot has more visual impact, can contain larger plants or groups of plants and is less likely to get knocked or blown over. And the larger the pot, the less quickly the compost dries out in hot weather, and the less vulnerable the roots are to hard frost.

A large pot can become a nucleus,

spawning a cluster of smaller pots round its base: closely grouped plants create a favourably humid microclimate and shelter each other from wind and weather. Groups of pots may vary in size and shape, but they shouldn't vary enormously in materials and aspirations.

With terracotta pots, make sure the clay used is frost-proof. Some clays spall or crack if saturated, then frozen: growing ivy over the rim and down the side of a pot protects the most vulnerable parts from water. Saucers are necessary for balconies, roof terraces or patios with wooden decking, quarry tiles or carpet tiles and for absolutely pristine gardens; remember to clean out regularly the leaves, slime, slugs and woodlice which tend to collect in outdoor saucers.

Like pots, window boxes are available in a wide variety of materials and styles. Again, the larger the better. A minimum depth of 17 centimetres (7 inches) is needed, to allow for 2.5 centimetres (1 inch) of drainage material at the bottom, and 2.5 centimetres (1 inch) between the surface of the compost and the rim for watering. The box should be fixed firmly in position, whether you are resting it on a wide sill or supporting it on steel angle brackets. Hooks and safety chains from the box to the adjacent wall are a good idea, especially if it is positioned above ground-floor level.

Plastic and PVC window boxes are easily available. They are not beautiful, but the darker ones are much less obtrusive than white and light green boxes (although you could get away with white on a white windowsill). The best approach with plastic window boxes is to camouflage them with trailing plants. If the box is visible from inside, then a

Above *Oriental restraint: dark glazed containers allow plants to shine, indoors or out. A mixture of hardy evergreens and not-quite-hardy azalea enjoy rubbing shoulders outdoors in summer; their destinations differ during the winter months.*

Left *A raised, internal planting bed against a window offers endless opportunities for spatial puns. Here, the mellow brick moving smoothly from exterior to interior continues the pun, and a tender climber makes full use of the available sunlight.*

double deception will be necessary; fill the inside sill with plants in pretty containers.

Terracotta, wood and glass-fibre 'lead' window boxes are usually more attractive, and more expensive. Make sure wooden ones are either pressure impregnated or made of a hardwood such as oak or elm. Reproduction boxes and those in a period style should be approached with care. Obviously, an ornate 'Victorian' window box on a Victorian house is fine, and it may even work well on a modern building, but the same box could be disastrous on a 1930s house. Whichever style and material you choose, the window boxes should be empathetic to the building and to the other containers in the garden.

Outdoor hanging baskets and wall-mounted pots need have little personality of their own, as their role is to be concealed with plants. There is still a certain amount of exposure in early summer, however, when annuals and bedding plants are small, and out of season.

Traditional wire hanging baskets and wall-mounted half baskets are unobtrusive; line them with dark fibrous mats which are far nicer than the black polythene often used and are easier to find than sphagnum moss. Terracotta, plastic-covered steel and wrought-iron hanging baskets are more expensive, and range from the attractive to the ugly. Solid plastic hanging baskets fitted with drip trays are undeniably practical but rather ugly and, because plants can't be tucked into the sides as they are in a traditional wire basket, plant growth is slow to conceal the pot.

Baskets tend to look best in a natural architectural context: an entrance porch, overhanging roof or deep window reveals. Hanging baskets from wall brackets can

also be attractive as long as they are not dotted about at random. If they are close to a window or door the baskets give indoor pleasure as well: always consider how they will look from both the outside and the inside. Fixed on either side of a window, flower-filled hanging baskets frame a view. Ten hanging baskets in a tight row can turn a blank wall opposite a window into a focal point. Three over a tall window, filled with morning glories, black-eyed Susans or trailing nasturtiums, would be like a summer curtain; filled with shorter plants, such as petunia, alyssum or lobelia, the effect would be that of a pelmet of flowers and greenery.

A UNIFIED APPROACH TO PLANTING

Co-ordinating garden plants on a wall, in a window box or hanging basket, with the various colour schemes of individual rooms is possible, but quite difficult to get right. Most people consider the planting immediately next to a house as it is seen from the outside, and rightly so. A Mediterranean villa covered with a sheet of purple bougainvillea or a house covered with a winter-flowering yellow jasmine is so strikingly beautiful that whether the flowers match the various colour schemes inside is of little significance.

If all the window boxes on a house façade are filled with the same plants or same combination of plants the result is bound to be visually coherent. On a rendered white wall, try tightly packed wallflowers in autumn, opening deep-wine red in spring, followed by pale and deep-pink hanging geraniums in summer. On a dark red brick façade, strike a cool note with white tulips, pale blue forget-me-nots, and ice-grey variegated ivy in spring, with silvery-white bush honeysuckle and silver-leaved cineraria replacing the tulips and forget-me-nots in summer. You could repeat the plant 'recipe' in tubs or pots.

In multi-family dwellings, a unified approach to façade planting is not always possible and designing window boxes and hanging baskets room-by-room is fair game. Even then, it is nice to have skeletal evergreen planting, such as ivy, in all the containers, with the flowers changing to match the rooms. Try repeating the same plants on the inside windowsill or on a nearby table. Some window boxes are attractive enough to be repeated indoors as well: as with plants, never assume that a container sold for outdoor use has to be used outdoors.

Doubling up the imagery of spring bulbs, summer annuals or winter evergreens on both sides of a pane of glass is a good idea. Buy twice the number of bedding geraniums, busy Lizzies or begonias necessary for a window box, and arrange the extra plants along the inside windowsill. Looking out, when the window is open on a warm, still day, is like being outside. At night, when the room is lit, the doubling-up effect can be enjoyed from the outside as well.

Picking flowers or foliage from a window box for indoors has to be done with great restraint if the window box is to remain attractive. You can cheat by buying cut daffodils to mass in front of a daffodil-filled window box or cut tulips in front of a tulip-filled one. Augmenting cut sweet peas, china asters or pot marigolds from a window box with bunches bought from a florist can add weight to the inevitable thinness of a window-box display.

THE PLANTS

Choosing what to plant nearest a house is subject to many of the same guidelines as choosing indoor plants. Avoid the 'one of each' approach: a window box filled with white, yellow, pink, blue and red hyacinths in equal measure may have something to please everybody, but less overall impact than a window box filled with hyacinths of a single colour.

Ideally, a basic 'core' planting of evergreens should be supplemented with plants that add temporary colour and interest. Or, if you consider bare earth or compost the enemy of successful 'view-out' gardening but have no real interest in gardening as an ongoing activity, use evergreens alone. A tidy row of box or dwarf conifers in a sunny window box, or spotted laurel and ivy in a shady one, is not innovative, but not temperamental or demanding either. There are low-growing evergreen plants for general ground cover: ivy, periwinkle, deadnettle, coral bells, lungwort, bugle, bergenia, *Pachysandra* and *Euphorbia robbiae*. You can still have touches of drama: camellia flowers are as showy as any annual, the berries of holly, cotoneaster and mahonia are seasonally attractive, and the long hanging catkins of *Garrya* could not be more exotic looking. Then, too, the green of evergreen hardy plants is as wide ranging as the green of house plants. And there are plenty of variegated evergreen hardy plants but, like variegated plants indoors, they should be used with restraint.

Evergrey can replace evergreen in sunny gardens. Lavender, cotton lavender, curry plant and *Senecio* 'Sunshine' can be combined with low-growing

Far left *Zonal pelargoniums move with consummate ease from house to garden, provided they are not exposed to frost. A deep windowsill and shutters provide an architectural setting for the clustered plants; if scattered about a garden, pelargoniums can look like abandoned litter.*

Left *A vignette in white and green, with white hydrangeas as the main characters. The doubled-up effect of hydrangeas on both sides of the window is obviously successful when seen from inside; whether it is equally pleasurable seen from the outside depends on the source and intensity of light, height above ground level and, ultimately, access.*

lamb's ears, pinks, arabis or alyssum. Evergrey plants tend to look tacky in bad winters, however, and most need annual hard pruning to keep them from becoming straggly and bare.

Long-term bulbs require just a little more effort than evergreens or evergreys. Snowdrops, winter-flowering iris, scillas, daffodils and many tulips can be left in the ground year after year, where they will increase in number. On the other hand, most take a long and ugly time dying down after flowering. While this doesn't matter in a wild garden or large garden, it does in the part of the garden viewed from the window. If you cut the leaves off, the bulbs won't flower the following year; if you tie the leaves in little knots, in an attempt to neaten them, they merely look peculiar. You could dig the bulbs up and heel them in an out-of-the-way part of the garden, or if the bulbs are growing in pots you can move them. The most ruthless and extravagant solution is to treat the bulbs as annuals, discarding them after flowering and replacing them the following year.

Herbaceous perennials, the most be-loved of plants, are also the hardest ones to accommodate near the house, because they spend most of the year out of flower and half the year below ground. Planting snowdrops, winter-flowering iris, crocus, *Chionodoxa* or winter aconites with herbaceous perennials, such as del-phiniums, lupins and peonies, gives a two-season display, but even then, there will be vacant, boring stretches in be-tween. Those with large gardens can pot up herbaceous perennials coming into flower, move them to a position near the house where they can be seen from a

Above *House plants moved outdoors for the summer months can be given a summer wardrobe. Use the bare compost for such fleeting annuals as lobelia, alyssum, or, as here, busy Lizzie. When frost threatens, move the whole display indoors, to get a few extra weeks' enjoyment.*

Right *A hot courtyard is home for wall plants and a trio of cypress, topped with a collection of herbs.*

window, and then return them to the open ground. Those without that luxury have to improvise. You could buy three, four or five young hostas, for example, and pot them in a single large container. But as well as being an expensive exercise, some perennials don't flower the first year they are planted, and even five young plants won't equal the glory of a well established clump.

In spring, plant stalls at fêtes often sell huge clumps of herbaceous perennials, by-products of a lifting and dividing process in someone's garden. As well as hosta, look for clumps of day lily, African lily, arum lily, lady's mantle, astilbe, bear's breeches, hardy geranium and *Iris sibirica*. Carefully remove as much of the soil from the roots as you can, then pot the clumps in fresh compost. Keep the pots well watered and position them so they are visible from the house. If you have nowhere to store the plants at the end of the season, return them to an autumn fête or give them to a friend with a garden.

There are so many pretty annuals from which to choose, that it is more a question of how to use them than which ones. However, certain annuals – ageratums, salvias, French and African marigolds and wax begonias – seem to mingle less easily with their neighbours than others. This is partly due to their rigidly erect or compact forms, and partly due to the way they are traditionally used: bedded out like a row of unstrung pearls. Especially near the house, aim for a generous, even slightly crowded, effect, not a series of isolated plants presiding over a background of compost. The planting distances given on seed packets and in most gardening books are the horticulturally ideal ones: each annual plant is treated as a potentially

perfect specimen needing space between it and its neighbours. Planted closer together, annuals become a fabric of colour, fully clothing pots, window boxes or the open ground.

As with bulbs, single-colour themes for annuals are safe and popular: white pelargoniums, white petunias and white lobelia, for example, or blue kingfisher daisies, blue lobelia and petunias. Pleasant, too, are the three-colour schemes, such as the traditional blue lobelia, pink ivy-leaved geranium and white petunia. Multi-colour schemes can be successful, as long as the colours are not used regimentally, in humourless formal patterns – such schemes are best reserved for municipal parks where they can be impressive simply because of the grand scale.

House plants, moved out for the summer, can become the basis for two-tier seasonal displays. Large indoor trees, such as palm, standard citrus, *Heptapleurum* and oleander, can have lobelia, nasturtium, busy Lizzie, alyssum, Livingstone daisy, petunia or even snippets of ivy planted in the bare compost round the edge of the pot. They won't hurt an established plant, and a fortnightly feed with general-purpose liquid fertilizer ensures enough nutrients to go round. By the end of summer, a mass of flowers and foliage will have hidden all the compost. Bring the plants indoors when frost threatens, and they will continue to flower, given good light. (Spray the lot with insecticide first, so you don't bring pests indoors as well.) Remove and discard them as soon as they start to wither, filling any space left by their root balls with fresh compost.

This two-tier summer treatment works equally well with smaller, short-term

house plants, especially those that are leggy or bare at the base. Add white lobelia to a pot of bright red geraniums, or train annual morning glory up a *Dizygotheca*. Variegated abutilon often goes bare at the base; if you haven't the heart to cut it back, use it to support bright orange and yellow climbing nasturtiums, or climbing black-eyed Susans. At the end of the summer, you can move the show indoors, as above, then discard the lot when the annuals have finished.

The kitchen window box and window-sill are often recommended as suitable places for growing vegetables. So, too, are pots outside the kitchen door. It is easy to understand the appeal behind this idea, but alas it is easier said than done. A minimum window box or pot depth of 25 centimetres (10 inches) is needed, as well as direct sunlight. If you have these, you could grow dwarf bush tomatoes or dwarf beans, both of which are pretty plants and can be harvested without ruining their appearance. Aubergines and peppers are not particularly attractive, and tend to crop poorly outdoors in temperate climates. Ornamental cabbage ceases being ornamental the moment it is harvested, and the same is true for 'Salad-Bowl' crinkle-edged lettuce.

Window-box/windowsill herb gardens make more sense. So does growing strawberries: their foliage, flowers and fruit are pretty, and the plants are cheap enough to

Honeysuckle, with the support of Boston ivy and clematis, frames the entrance to a home, providing flowers, fragrance and foliage. When the honeysuckle and clematis finish, the Boston ivy steals the show, with its brilliant autumn foliage.

discard at the end of the season without guilt. Strawberries make a pleasant change from bedding plants, especially when their runners are allowed to arch over the rim of the window box, or are tied vertically to canes or trellis work. Even with strawberries, if the kitchen window is on the front façade of the house, it may be more important to have all the window boxes planted consistently than to have an edible window-box garden.

There are several ways to avoid empty containers in winter-time. Instead of evergreen plants, consider using wallflowers. If they are healthy, well-grown and densely planted, wallflowers have a powerful winter presence, even out of flower. Like all biennials, they can go in as soon as annuals come out, in mid-autumn. Double daisies, pansies, primulas and forget-me-nots are smaller than wallflower plants in autumn, and they make little winter impact. The tall flower spikes of foxgloves and Canterbury bells make these biennials more suitable for tubs and large pots than window boxes; by autumn, both plants have made good-sized leaf rosettes. Large pots of either beside a door or a cool, sunny entrance hall would make a lovely early summer show.

An unorthodox approach is to treat window boxes like outdoor vases. Tightly 'plant' the window boxes with vertical branches of red- or yellow-barked dogwood, alder, birch, beech or bright green kerria. Out in the cold, and watered from time to time, these window-box 'shrub gardens' will last the winter, and, chances are, the dogwood and kerria may have started sending out roots by spring. Shorter-lived, but equally effective, are tightly packed branches of evergreens treated the same way: holly, spotted laurel, rhodo-

dendron, Portuguese laurel, laurustinus, brightly coloured elaeagnus, and evergreen cotoneaster in berry or conifer branches are just a few possibilities. They may need replacing after a month or six weeks, but, even if you have to buy the branches, it will be money well spent. These 'instant shrubs' can be any height you like, as long as the stems are deep enough in the compost to provide stability. The branches can be left in their informal state, or clipped into formal 'hedges'. This system combines well with autumn-planted tulips, hyacinths or daffodils: remove the branches around winter solstice to give the bulbs room to grow.

GOOD SCENTS

Doors, windows, window boxes and scented plants should be inseparable. There are many plants that combine delicious fragrance with attractive form, and doubly earn their keep. On a large, sunny wall try a heavily scented climbing rose, such as the deep crimson climbing 'Etoile de Holland', the pale yellow Old Glory rose 'Gloire de Dijon', or the blush-white 'Mme Alfred Carriere' which tolerates light shade. While roses and scent are almost synonymous, some clematis are scented too: the spring-flowering *Clematis montana* has scent reminiscent of vanilla, and the cowslip-scented *Clematis rehderana* carries its yellow, bell-shaped flowers in summer and autumn. Of the honeysuckles, *Lonicera japonica halliana* is both heavily scented and, in mild winters, evergreen. The flowers of wisteria are elusively fragrant, making this the obligatory climber trained round so many cottage doors and windows. Another

cottage-garden trick is to grow one climber up through another to double the seasonal pleasure – a spring-flowering clematis through a summer-flowering rose, for example.

Scented shrubs for container or wall-growing include Mexican orange, myrtle, broom, daphne, lavender and some viburnums, such as *V.* × *burkwoodii* and *V. carlesii*. Pots of scented lilies next to a door make entering or leaving a pleasure: highly scented lilies include the gold-rayed lily, the Japanese lily and *Lilium formosanum*, all at their best in late summer and early autumn. In early summer, display pots of Madonna lilies (*L. candidum*). Datura, or angel's trumpet, should be grown in a pot so it can be moved indoors for winter; it has a powerful night scent and white or scarlet and yellow flowers.

Even a window box can be a splendid source of scent. Sweet Williams, wallflowers, crocus, narcissi, hyacinths and polyanthus can fill the air with spring fragrance. Summer options include annual carnations, scented-leaved geraniums, stocks (both day- and night-scented), heliotrope, petunias, tobacco plants and sweet peas. With sweet peas, it is the tall-growing, small-flowered 'Grandiflora' type that produces the most intense fragrance; of the 'window-box', dwarf forms, the multi-coloured 'Patio' and the two-toned pink 'Cupid' are the best for scent.

Tiniest of all the scented plants are the creeping herbs that release scent when walked on. Tuck creeping thyme, pennyroyal or creeping mint into spaces between paving stones in an entrance area for well-timed fragrance, especially on hot, sunny days. Remember, also, that violet foliage (*Viola odorata*) emits a haunting fragrance on a mild, humid day.

Left *A tiny, private Eden. Hardy and tender plants; formally trained and exuberantly informal ones; flowering and foliage plants; potted and open grown plants completely obscure neighbouring houses and the outside world.*

Above *A one-off, indoor-outdoor garden, in which carpeting plants are encouraged to meander at will. Creating a 'wild' garden indoors demands skill in selecting and maintaining the plants, and a* laissez-faire *attitude as long as the plants keep within the allotted space.*

HOW TO

For some people, looking after house plants is a raison d'être – *the horticultural equivalent of raising children or pets. But the vast majority of house plant owners find detailed horticultural information confusing, boring and irrelevant; they simply want to know enough to get by.*

House plants can be regarded coldly, as cut flowers with roots, to be enjoyed for their brief beauty and discarded the instant that beauty palls. Indeed, certain plants – chrysanthemums and poinsettias, for example – are best treated like this, although their lives can be extended several weeks. Huge potted lilies are another example; their out-of-season treatment requires a garden or greenhouse and continuing care for fifty weeks, for the reward of perhaps two weeks' display.

As a general rule, the more expensive a house plant, the more sensible it is to do some research into its needs and expected lifespan before buying it. Some very short-lived plants can be very expensive: large azaleas, bougainvilleas and gardenias, for example, rarely make it from one year to the next as house plants, although they are exquisite and undeniably tempting when in flower. Knowing how long you can expect the plant to live and the conditions in which it will survive best are prerequisites for a happy relationship, however long or short.

As with raising children, raising house plants involves a certain amount of benign neglect, and a relatively relaxed attitude.

More plants are killed by too much care than too little, in terms of water, feeding and fussing generally. Garden centres sell scientific instruments for measuring the moisture content of the compost in a flower pot, and others for measuring the nutrient content of the compost. While these are useful in controlled laboratory conditions, they are less so in the home. Understanding the natural life cycle and rhythms of plants, backed with a modicum of knowledge of the plant's origin, is all you need.

An attractively arranged 'photosession' display of leaf, stem and softwood cuttings prepared for propagation. However fascinating the scientific process is, in reality the paraphernalia associated with plant propagation is modest looking at best. Considered purely in terms of interior design, baby plants, or bits of plants in the process of forming roots, frequently have little to offer.

LIGHTING

All plants need light to live, and some need more than others. Indoors, the intensity of light can be very deceptive and varies enormously from one part of a room to another. An area that appears to be reasonably light may be too dark for some plants, and far too bright for others. A window or glazed door is the usual source of natural light in a room; the intensity of light depends on whether it is obscured by nearby trees or buildings, on what season it is and on the direction the window faces. South-facing windows receive the most hours of direct sunlight, with those facing south-west and south-east receiving slightly less (it is, of course, the opposite in the Southern Hemisphere). In summer, the light rays enter at a steep angle, illuminating the area directly in front of the window. In winter, the low rays enter the room almost horizontally; they are weaker, but extend farther into the room. An east-facing window gets morning light: very little indeed in winter, but a great deal in the summer months, although even then, the sun's rays will no longer reach the window by the time they have built up their noon-day intensity. West-facing windows get the evening light: again, very little in winter but quite strong in the summer months. Windows facing due north (or south in the Southern Hemisphere) get no direct light but have a relatively even supply of indirect light throughout the year.

By the time the natural light flowing into a room is 1.8 metres (6 feet) or so from the window, very little of it is actually usable by a plant, although white interiors and mirrors reflect the light and are more helpful than light-absorbing colours. Ironically, placing plants on either side of a window in the hope of giving them a sunny home can have the opposite effect: the deeper the sills, the more shadowed these places will be.

In temperate climates, commercial growers rely on vast banks of artificial lights to supplement, or completely replace, natural light. Unfortunately, the lighting systems used in homes do little to help plants. Incandescent light gives out most of its energy as heat; for such light to have any beneficial effect, it would have to be so close to a plant that the heat would scorch its leaves. Fluorescent lights are generally more beneficial to plant growth, but these, too, have to be quite close to the plants – no more than 60 centimetres (2 feet) away – to be effective. As fluorescent light gives out relatively little heat, there is no problem with scorching, but the proximity of the lighting fixture may well detract from the plants. Whether fitted into reflective casings and hung on chains above eye-level or fitted directly into a wall or ceiling, the tubing will be visible and may not fit comfortably within the room; those designed especially to promote plant growth emit violet-blue and red light, creating a red glow, which may also prove disconcerting. Mercury vapour lights are beneficial to plants and are effective some distance away, but have very high wattage and therefore are quite costly to run.

Desert cacti and succulents generally require the most light all year round. So do variegated plants and those with bright purple foliage, to make up for the small amount of chlorophyll in their leaves. Plants with silver or grey leaves, and those with waxy or woolly leaf surfaces, also tend to require bright light – all of these characteristics developed as a defence against the heat, bright light and drought of their native environments.

Because plants grow towards the light, they will eventually become lopsided if they are grown on a windowsill or, indeed, anywhere else in a room where the source of light is strongly directional. To overcome this problem, turn the plants round – either a half or quarter turn – every few days.

HEATING

The maximum and minimum temperatures in a room, together with the quality of light, are what determines whether a particular plant is suitable for a particular environment. Very few of us, though, will alter the room temperature to meet the needs of a plant; you will either buy a plant regardless of its temperature requirements and hope for the best, or make an effort to match the plant selected to the existing temperature. In most homes, this means 18 to 24°C (65 to 75°F), the normal temperature range of a centrally heated house. Plants from semi-tropical and tropical climates, rather than those from the cooler temperate ones, are therefore the safest choices, especially in the winter months.

Unfortunately, many of the most popular house plants are from temperate climates, and prefer winter temperatures in the region of 7 to 10°C (45 to 50°F). These include aspidistra, jasmine, cyclamen, chrysanthemum, azalea, hydrangea, fuchsia, ivy, oleander, pelargonium, primula, cineraria, forced bulbs and most ferns. Oddly enough, desert cacti need

Winter light

With its low angle, winter light penetrates farther into a room, and can be far more worrying to the eyes, than summer light. Winter light is also dispersed over a larger area, but it is intrinsically weaker in intensity, and the farther from the window, the weaker it becomes.

Summer light

With the high summer sun, light enters a room at a steep angle and consequently lights a small area very near the window. It is intrinsically stronger in intensity than winter light and, when combined with the solar gain through glass, can scorch delicate foliage and flowers.

cool winter temperatures, to discourage spindly and lank growth in response to the low light levels. The European fan palm, Chinese fan palm, desert fan palm, Canary date palm, lady palm and windmill palm also prefer cool winter temperatures. None of these plants will collapse and die overnight from excessive heat, but their lives will be inevitably shortened.

Lowering the temperature at night by about 4°C (10°F) is one way of counteracting the problem of excessive winter heat; providing high humidity is another (but, remember, mist-spraying a plant to provide a moist atmosphere can harm nearby furniture and perpetual condensation does not do the structural fabric of the house much good, either). Damping down, the process of spraying the floor and staging of a greenhouse to increase humidity, obviously is impractical in most rooms. Instead, you can stand the plant pot on a shallow dish or bowl filled with gravel or pebbles and topped with water; the water slowly evaporates into the atmosphere, creating a humid microclimate around the plant. Large plastic or zinc windowsill trays are ideal. Several pots can be placed on the gravel. However, a humid microclimate doesn't work for desert cacti and succulents, which will rot.

Summer heat is far less problematic. Opening windows to increase ventilation is normal at this time, and this is beneficial to plants too, as long as they are not in a direct draught. Increased humidity is, again, helpful.

Whatever the temperature range a plant will tolerate, sudden and dramatic fluctuations are nearly always damaging. A temperature change of 8°C (20°F) during the course of a day is the maximum most house plants will tolerate.

Feeding time

Foliar feeds are quick acting – good for starved plants or those with small root systems.

Slow-release fertilizer sticks should be placed well away from roots; they can burn.

Nutrient-impregnated pads placed under the pots slowly release nutrients when wet.

Fertilizer pellets should be pushed well into the soil with a pencil, dibber or screwdriver.

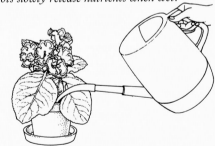

Diluted liquid or powdered fertilizer is the most common method of feeding plants.

When using granular fertilizer, over-feeding is a risk. Follow the maker's instructions.

FEEDING

Plants should be fed at certain times of the year, and not at others. 'Starved' has connotations of cruelty, but in fact it is far crueller to feed a plant during its natural dormancy. Tropical plants grow in their native environment all year round, because the heat and light levels remain constantly high. In a temperate climate (unless artificial light is provided), even tropical plants should be induced to rest during the winter months.

Feed a plant when it is growing actively; this is usually in spring and summer, but not always. Christmas cactus and cyclamen, for example, need feeding in the depths of winter, which is normally when they flower. As well as flowers, other signs of active growth include new shoots, leaves and fruit. Newly bought or newly potted plants should not need feeding initially, even in the growing season, because there should be sufficient nutrients for the first month in the case of peat-based composts, and for the first two to three months in loam-based composts. Too much food can cause weak, vulnerable growth, and can also build up as salts in the compost, scorching the roots. On the other hand, if a newly purchased plant has pale, unnaturally small or brown-edged leaves, if it is meant to be flowering but isn't, or if it shows no sign of growth in the growing season, begin feeding.

In the growing season feed quick-growing plants weekly and slow-growing plants once every two weeks. Concentrated liquid or water-soluble fertilizer, diluted and then watered on to the compost, is a very convenient method. These fertilizers work best if the compost is already slightly moist. Other alternatives include fertilizer-impregnated pads placed between the pot and its saucer; when watered from below, nutrients are slowly released and drawn into the compost. Slow-release fertilizer 'spikes' are expensive, but once inserted supply nutrients for up to six months: a large plant in a big pot may need several spikes, while one is sufficient for a small plant. Insert spikes against the inner edge of the pot, as any roots coming into direct contact with them are liable to be scorched.

Foliar feeds are sprayed directly on to the leaves, and are absorbed more quickly than those taken up through the roots. Foliar feeding is most effective for plants with relatively small root systems, such as bromeliads, epiphytic cacti and ferns, and for plants that have not been fed sufficiently for some time. It can damage nearby furnishings, so move the plant into the garden or into a sink or bath first.

Most plants respond adequately to a balanced general fertilizer – that is, one that contains roughly equal proportions of nitrates, phosphates and potash, and tiny amounts of certain minerals or trace elements. Commercial growers may change the feeding routine of a plant several times during the course of its growing season, and there are specialized formulae available: those high in nitrates, recommended for foliage plants and for most plants at the beginning of the growing season; those high in phosphates, for flowering plants in bud and flower; and those high in potash, to help plants that have finished flowering to build up strength for the following year. 'Acid' fertilizers have chelated iron added for acid-loving plants, such as stephanotis.

The golden rule about fertilizers is: if in doubt, underfeed rather than overfeed.

WATERING

Watering and feeding are interrelated. House plants need water and food most when they are actively growing, usually when temperatures and light levels are high. The quantity of water and the frequency and method of watering depend on several factors. Plants originating from tropical rain forests; large plants and those with large, thin leaves; plants that are kept pot-bound deliberately, and those growing in large pots, clay pots or peat-based composts all need generous watering. Plants that come from hot, dry climates; those with fleshy, succulent growth; those that have recently been potted on or re-potted, and those growing in loam-based composts or plastic pots will need less water relatively.

Of course these guidelines can be contradictory: in the case of a newly potted, large-leaved plant in loam-based compost and a clay pot, for example. Here, you would need to take a more simplistic approach (although there are inevitable exceptions). In the growing season, the compost should not be allowed to dry out completely, nor should it be perpetually moist. Think about watering when the top 6 millimetres ($\frac{1}{4}$ inch) of compost is dry; water thoroughly, using water at room temperature, and water again only when the compost starts to dry out. Feel the surface of the compost with your fingers, pressing down lightly. If it feels dry, water. Day-time watering is preferable to evening watering, when the temperature falls and dreaded fungal infections are liable to strike.

There are many signs indicating a dry compost. It is much lighter in weight, and usually in colour, than a wet compost. A clay pot holding dry compost will make a hollow, ringing sound if tapped; if the compost is moist, the sound will be a dull thud. Peat-based compost that has shrunk away from the sides of the pot indicates a very dry compost indeed and calls for emergency response: the pot should be placed in a bucket or sink filled with water, and left until air bubbles stop appearing.

The plants themselves have various ways of showing that they need water: wilting, dropping their flower buds and lower leaves or in extreme cases, all their leaves, and producing unnaturally short-lived flowers or shrivelled-up growth. Unfortunately, many of these symptoms can have other causes: extreme temperature fluctuation, for example, can cause buds to drop. As with feeding, it is generally safer to give a plant too little water than too much.

Watering can be done from above or from below. Either fill the space between the rim of the pot and the surface of the compost with water, allowing it to soak through, and then repeat, if necessary; or stand the pot on a saucer or shallow dish filled with water and leave for thirty minutes. Any water left standing in the saucer or dish should be removed. Watering from below is better for plants with hairy or waxy leaves or succulent growth, and those with corms vulnerable to rotting.

Tap water containing calcium, or 'hard' water, can be a problem for lime-hating house plants, such as azalea. Boiling the water removes some of the calcium; applying chelated iron helps counteract the build-up of calcium in the compost (follow the manufacturer's instructions). Purists collect rain water for watering such plants, but this isn't always practicable.

SEASONAL CARE

Generally, the low light levels and low temperatures of a temperate-climate winter cause a plant's natural activity to be reduced. Growth slows down, transpiration (loss of water through the leaves) is reduced, and water and nutrient needs are reduced accordingly. Most house plants would continue to grow if fed and watered generously during the winter months, especially if grown in centrally heated conditions, but because of the low light levels, this growth would be weak and vulnerable to all manner of pests and diseases. Plants from temperate regions would be additionally weakened, being deprived of their natural dormancy period. During the spring and summer months, with increased light levels and increased temperatures, most plants grow actively, requiring more nutrients and watering and, if tropical or semi-tropical in origin, increased humidity. Pests and diseases also tend to become active during these warm, light months, having overwintered in a dormant state, so constant vigilance is required, especially in spring, to keep them under control.

As well as the seasonal cycle, there is the flowering cycle. When plants flower is largely determined by the hours of light and darkness in a day. 'Short-day' plants, such as tender cyclamen, winter-flowering iris, snowdrops, poinsettias and chrysanthemums, are triggered into flowering by at least two months of long nights and short days. (That potted chrysanthemums can be had all year round is a tribute to growers' ingenuity; they artificially black out and light greenhouses over many weeks to 'trick' the plants into

flowering.) Plants in flower do need feeding and watering, whatever the season, although they should have a little less in cool temperatures than in warm ones. Some plants – tender cyclamen, again – rest during the summer months and all watering should cease then.

Many plants benefit from being stood out of doors during the summer months, where those that are sun-loving can get increased doses of light, and sun- and shade-lovers alike get unlimited 'ventilation'. Shelter is essential, as wind can scorch and brown the foliage, and many house plants, especially those with thin leaves, need protection from strong direct sunlight in the hottest months of the year. Very few house plants can take the direct sunlight in a south-facing window over the summer months (north-facing in the Southern hemisphere); it is much hotter than a similar position outdoors. Either move the plants away from the light, or protect them with translucent curtains or slatted blinds.

FORCING BULBS

Tulip, hyacinth and daffodil can be forced into bloom much earlier than their natural flowering time and are often sold specially prepared (pre-refrigerated) for this purpose. Although snowdrop, winter aconite, chionodoxa, grape hyacinth, scilla, dwarf iris, crocus and fritillary cannot be rushed by special preparation or very warm temperatures, they will bloom a bit earlier indoors than outdoors and of course the blooms won't be damaged by weather. Plant the bulbs almost touching each other. Do this as early in autumn as possible, to give them time to form good root

Forcing hyacinths

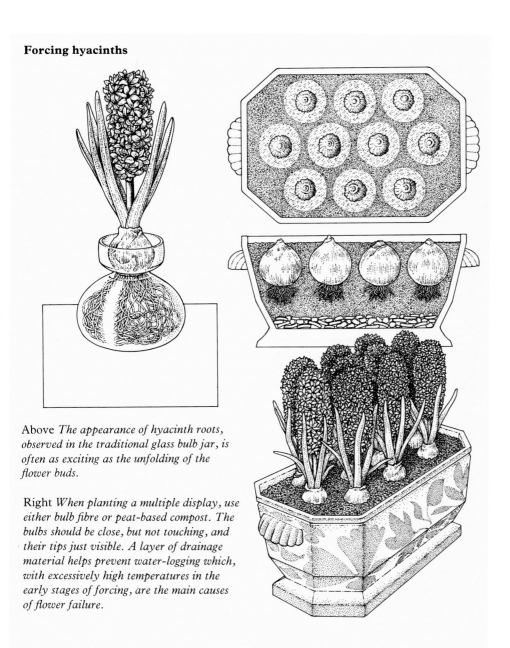

Above *The appearance of hyacinth roots, observed in the traditional glass bulb jar, is often as exciting as the unfolding of the flower buds.*

Right *When planting a multiple display, use either bulb fibre or peat-based compost. The bulbs should be close, but not touching, and their tips just visible. A layer of drainage material helps prevent water-logging which, with excessively high temperatures in the early stages of forcing, are the main causes of flower failure.*

On holiday

Place plants directly on capillary matting with one end resting in a water-filled sink. The water is absorbed by the matting and is taken up by the compost (and then the plant's roots) through the drainage holes in the pots.

systems. Leave the growing tips of tulips, hyacinths and daffodils exposed; cover the others with their own depth of fibre. Water lightly, then leave for at least six weeks in a cold, dark, but frost-free, place, with a maximum temperature of 9°C (48°F). Keep the compost just moist. Once new shoots are visible you can move the container into a slightly warmer, shady spot for a week or two, then into the warmth and light of a normal room. You can have a much longer display by preparing several containers: the planted bulbs will come to no harm if left in the cold and dark for a month after the new shoots have formed, so you can bring in a new pot each week to begin flowering when the previous pot has finished. If you don't have anywhere cool and dark to bring bulbs on, you can always cheat by buying bulbs in bud or flower.

HOLIDAY CARE

There is nothing like a reliable friend or neighbour to look after your plants when necessary. (If you have large numbers of house plants, perhaps even a greenhouse or conservatory, you could form a plant-sitting co-operative with like-minded friends.) Moving a plant out of direct sunlight and watering it thoroughly immediately before the holiday may be sufficient when you are away for a short time and there are no suitable plant sitters to call on. Otherwise, any of the following measures may prove helpful.

In autumn, winter or spring, reducing the temperature of the house to 10°C (50°F), or even a few degrees lower, reduces transpiration and thus the need for water. Keeping plants tightly grouped

Camping out

Except for plants with grey, hairy, waxy or woolly foliage, a transparent plastic bag makes a perfect holiday environment.

helps conserve moisture, especially if they are placed on trays or shallow bowls of gravel topped up with water. Moving all the house plants into the bathroom, placing them in gravel and water-filled containers, and filling the bath with water, will create a moist atmosphere: internal, windowless bathrooms are not very suitable, however, as plants need natural light, especially over a week or more. On a smaller scale, thoroughly watering a plant and then enclosing it in a clear plastic bag suspended on bamboo sticks or canes

creates an equally humid environment (but place the enclosed plant well away from direct sunlight, or it will suffer death by steaming).

Capillary matting is useful for several small plants in plastic pots. The matting is best placed on the draining board of the kitchen sink, with one end resting in the water-filled sink. Leave the pots directly on the matting; the compost takes up water through the drainage holes.

There are more complicated trickle systems available, in which tubes slowly release water from a central reservoir into several plant containers. Sophisticated models have sensor valves that measure the moisture content in the compost and release additional water as necessary.

If, in spite of all efforts, the plants are found to be dried out, completely immerse the pot in a sink or bucket of tepid water, and leave it there until air bubbles stop rising. Thoroughly wet the foliage as well, using a mist spray if the plant is too big to be submerged.

Plants have an amazing will to survive and often the roots of a plant seemingly killed by drought (or frost) will eventually send up new growth. It can take years, however, for such a plant to reach its previous stature. During the intervening period, it may have little or no beauty at all, and whether the long wait is worth the trouble and care is a personal decision.

PRUNING

While some plants obviously have the capacity for rampant growth in their native environment and may perhaps grow with similar speed in the ideal conditions of a greenhouse or conservatory, few grow

quickly or excessively large in the confines of a normal room. In fact, most grow very slowly, remain the same size, or somehow contrive to shrink. In the unlikely event of a house plant growing too big for the house, it is more sensible to give it away than to cut it back. In terms of interior design, the larger a house plant is, provided it is healthy and well grown, the more impact it has.

There are occasions, though, when cosmetic pruning is called for. Pinching, or pinching out – when the tip or tips of certain plants are removed – encourages the dormant growth buds immediately behind it to become active and form side shoots. Pinching out may only involve 6 millimetres ($\frac{1}{4}$ inch) of growth being removed, hardly noticeable, but the end result will be a bushier, and often more free-flowering, plant. Fuchsias and pelargoniums are both vastly improved by regular pinching out – the process will have been carried out several times already by the commercial grower before the plants are even sold – and so too are busy Lizzie, wandering Jew, shrimp plant and zebrina. There is no point pinching out house plants that don't produce new growth from leaf nodes. Palms, bromeliads, ferns, cacti and plants that send up foliage directly from a rhizome (aspidistra, for instance) are all unsuitable.

Pinching out can take place at any time of year, but is most effective if done when plants are just starting into growth – usually early spring. It is a continuing process, perhaps necessary three or four times during the course of the growing season, as side shoots form which may need pinching out, too. Thumb and forefinger are the traditional 'tools' used, as tip growth is usually quite soft. For harder, woodier growth, use scissors or a sharp knife, always cutting to just above a node or pair of nodes.

Harsher pruning – cutting back growth substantially – should only be done if the plant has become bare and leggy at the base, or if its balance has been disturbed by an excessively long or ungainly bit of growth. Hard pruning should also be done at the beginning of the growing season, using secateurs with two cutting edges, or a sharp knife. The harder the pruning, the more new growth will be sent out – given ideal conditions. Nurseries will cut back the main stems of Cape leadwort by half and its long, floppy side shoots to a couple of centimetres ($\frac{3}{4}$ inch) from the base, at the end of every winter. The result is decidedly ugly, but only for a short time; the ample source of light in a greenhouse, coupled with near-perfect watering and feeding routines, means that by the end of spring, new (and more free-flowering) growth will have replaced what was cut off. In the home, on the other hand, with less light to encourage new growth and less perfect horticultural routines, the new growth can be disappointing or even non-existent. Also, in nurseries, recently pruned plants might be moved to an out-of-the-way greenhouse. In most homes, however, the heavily pruned plants will have to remain visible.

Removing any shoots that form on the single stem, or 'leg', of a plant trained as a standard is essential. So is the removal of shoots producing all-green foliage on a variegated plant; if left alone, the all-green shoot would soon overtake the variegated growth, and the plant would revert.

Although it is not strictly pruning, removing faded, brown and otherwise damaged leaves, and damaged or dead wood, both improves the look of a plant and keeps it from falling prey to pests and diseases. Dead-heading, or removing faded flowers, is equally sensible; it keeps the plant looking good, prevents it wasting energy on seed formation and may encourage the production of more flowers.

PROPAGATION

Propagation is an endless source of fascination. Propagating plants can be so absorbing that you may give little thought to the finished product, and where you are going to put it.

The equipment associated with propagation is not terribly attractive. Although there are many well-designed heated propagating units, they really are far more suited to the greenhouse or out-of-the-way back room than to the living room or conservatory. Far more often, though, little snippets of plants struggle to form roots in water-filled yoghourt containers or algae-filled jars, lined up along kitchen windowsills. Various attempts have been made to turn glass or transparent plastic propagating units into *objets d'art*, but they don't work. Hollow globes or 'strawberries', partially perforated to allow cuttings to be stuck through and designed to be hung decoratively about the house, are impossible to clean and the inner surfaces quickly build up with slimy deposits, as harmful to the plants as they are ugly to look at.

Considered on their own, baby plants really hold little attraction. While a huge spider plant or mother of thousands, festooned with young plantlets in various stages of growth, can be glorious, one detached plantlet is simply lost in a room,

whatever the size. A large plant has much much more visual impact than the number of small plants that would equal it. (It might be better to forget propagation altogether in some cases; instead, buy several plants of the same type and pot them in one large container. In fact, this is a standard procedure among ornamental plant growers: large specimens of the weeping fig and kentia palm, for example, are often made up of one large plant set in the middle of the pot, with several smaller, younger plants grouped around it to camouflage its naturally sparse base.) A good-size clivia, for example, is instantly divisible into six or eight smaller but completely independent plants; the same is true for queen's tears, aspidistra and all the clump-forming cacti and succulents. But because it can be done, does not mean that it necessarily should, particularly when considered in terms of interior design.

Traditionally, the surface of the compost in a flower pot is kept clear; it makes the process of watering easier, and looks tidy. But as long as there is not a densely matted tangle of roots on, or just below, the surface of the compost, it can be used to start off new plants. Three or four tiny plantlets of mother of thousands, for example, can be tucked into the compost in a 20 centimetre (8 inch) pot that is already inhabited. In due course, they should grow large enough to overhang the pot's rim to produce runners, or stolons, with plantlets of their own at the tips. This works best if the pot in question holds a plant of largely vertical growth, ideally with a single main stem. Orange, lemon, kumquat or grapefruit trees, grown as standards, are good examples; so is oleander. Plants which are naturally horizontal in growth habit or completely fill the pot are not as good 'nursemaids'.

In time, the young plants may have to be moved into pots of their own, if they threaten to compete too strongly with their host plant, either visually or horticulturally. Some combinations, though, can remain on permanent display. A few sprigs of ivy, variegated or all-green, tucked into the compost of a potted bay tree, should quickly take root and eventually cover the surface with a pretty mat of foliage. In the longer term, it will spill over the rim of the pot and down the sides. The ivy may need judicious trimming to keep it under control, but the trimmings can then be used to start off another ivy colony elsewhere, or as part of a floral display. Other candidates suitable for starting off in this way include wandering Jew (*Tradescantia* and *Zebrina*), piggy-back plant, bryophyllum, spider plant, hen-and-chicken fern, callisias (which are similar in appearance to wandering Jew), baby's tears or a small-growing aloe such as *A. brevifolia*. It is important to match the cultivation needs of the plant to be propagated with those of its host. Aloes, for example, need relatively dry compost and full light; to plant them around the base of a moisture- and shade-loving fern would be pointless.

Just as certain plants make better 'nursemaids', there are some plants that are more likely to succeed when propagated in this way. Those that come equipped with roots already formed – plantlets, offsets or plants that can be divided into several rooted sections – are least risky. Tip cuttings of soft-stemmed plants that quickly send out roots from the nodes are also worth trying. Busy Lizzies, coleus and pelargoniums are good examples. Cuttings taken from harder, older stems of house plants tend to form roots slowly and need special conditions – bottom heat and high humidity – to do so, and so are best avoided. If you are taking soft tip cuttings, remove the lower leaves before burying half the stem in the compost. Place the cuttings around the inner edge of the pot, where the drainage is good and there is less competition with the roots of the established plant.

A vertical plant with a carpet of a second, complementary plant growing around its base is most attractive. All the paraphernalia used in propagation is dispensed with during the initial stages; the surface of the compost, never wildly attractive, is camouflaged, and foliage growing over the rim of a container has a visually softening effect. The clarity and strength of the grouping is likely to be dissipated if you grow several different types of plant around the base of a single host: to keep mixed planting of this sort from looking twee is quite an art, even if all the plants concerned are horticulturally suited to one another.

Cuttings of plants that root in water can be used for display as they root. Try 10–15 centimetre (4–6 inch) lengths of coleus, busy Lizzie, Madagascar periwinkle, begonia, ivy, oleander and pelargonium. There is no need for the container to have clinical overtones. It should be chosen with the decor of the room in mind, and kept meticulously clean. Change the water daily, and check the state of the cuttings. Sometimes one or two lower leaves die before the roots form. Remove the dead leaves. Likewise, be ruthless with the occasional cutting that rots instead of roots. (Make sure that there are no submerged leaves, which inevitably rot.)

One-pot nurseries

The easiest plants to propagate will send out roots as happily in the compost of an occupied flower pot as in a propagating unit. Here, mother of thousands and a citrus tree trained as a standard make a pleasing combination. In time, the baby plants can be moved into containers of their own, or left as a permanent 'ground cover'.

BUYING PLANTS

An early morning visit to a major whole-sale plant market will reveal vans and lorries ranging from the elitist and fashionable to the local corner shop. Later that day, the identical house plants appear on the shelves of various shops, at widely differing prices. The mark up is obviously greater for shops in expensive areas or those with aspirations – florists in prestigious hotel lobbies are notorious – and price increases of three or four times is not uncommon. Mass chain stores, which make bulk purchases of hundreds of thousands of house plants, have such a huge turnover that the profit margins are kept down and the prices are more reasonable. Market stalls have minimal overheads, and their plants are usually the least expensive.

House plants are subject to seasonal as well as market forces. Poinsettias the weeks after Christmas are like chocolate bunnies the week after Easter – available cheaply if you don't mind the jaded imagery. Comparison shopping is sensible, provided you know a healthy, promising plant, or a dud one, when you see one. Although amazingly cheap house plants are suspect, high cost is no guarantee that the plant is in top condition.

As with cut flowers, a flowering house plant with every flower open is at the peak of its display. If it is a cheap-and-cheerful throwaway, such as calceolaria or cineraria, and you want it for a dinner party that evening, you may not be bothered. If it is a long-term and expensive plant, such as a hoya, jasmine or clivia, and you are sure you can get it to blossom again in a year's time, perhaps it doesn't

matter. But if you want a relatively long-lasting display choose plants with plump buds as well as open flowers. Inspect the tops of potted chrysanthemums; ideally, there should be buds below the open flowers. If you find little stumps instead, then someone else has had the pleasure of the first flush of blossom, and what you see is all you'll get. Some flower stalks, such as those of cymbidium, go brown and wizened immediately behind the neck of ageing flowers.

Pre-wrapped house plants can be risky. With opaque paper, the condition of the lower leaves is impossible to assess. They may be wilted, yellowed or brown-edged, or absent altogether, or pest and disease ridden. (The latter is doubly dangerous, as the infections or infestations could spread to healthy plants at home.) The leaves may have been deprived of light and air for some days, and will look it once unwrapped. In extremes, they simply fall off once the paper is removed. House plants tightly wrapped in transparent plastic or polythene may suffer from a build up of moisture.

Some house plants, such as polyanthus or cinerarias, look very much alike in form. Two weeping figs of a similar size and price can vary a great deal in form and grace. If the house plants are in a tightly packed display, separate those under consideration out from the rest, and inspect them in the round. Some house plants are naturally bare legged, but those that should be clothed to the base with foliage and aren't, and those that are very one sided in their growth, should be avoided. They may recover in due course, with careful pinching out and controlled exposure to light, but there is no point in buying a ready-made problem.

A common mistake is to select house plants as if choosing basketball players, largely by height. A smaller but more nicely proportioned plant may make better design sense.

Buying plants from shop fronts or outdoor stalls is a risky business in cold weather. Most commercially grown house plants start life in the perfect, warm and totally controlled conditions of a greenhouse. Being moved to a cold windy environment often without any period of hardening off period, is a harsh transition, and one which can prove fatal. A few days spent in near freezing conditions followed by a spell in a hot, dry, centrally heated home adds to the fatality rate. Remember that plants suffering from exposure to cold don't always look ill, and it may be a while before the symptoms declare themselves.

The biggest risk and excitement of all is buying plants at the garden stalls of fêtes or bazaars. The labels are sometimes detailed and correct, more often roughly accurate, wildly inaccurate or missing. The helpers behind the stalls sometimes know about plants, other times, not.

Rare house plants, not normally commercially grown, sometimes appear at plant stalls, as do miniature, and instant, specialist collections: a dozen different cultivars of African violets donated by an African violet fanatic, or a tray of small cacti, grown and donated by a cacti man. Huge, old hoyas or Swiss cheese plants whose owners grew bored with them, are regular gifts to plant stalls. (These take on new life with re-potting and dusting.)

The two main pitfalls are inadvertently introducing pests and diseases to your own plants, and buying not yet rooted – though sold as rooted – cuttings. To remedy the former, a precautionary spray with a general-purpose insecticide is sensible. The latter must be viewed as the donor's enthusiasm for the cause overtaking horticultural reality. If the cuttings are in a good rooting compost, they may root in due course; if not re-pot in peat-based compost, and hope for the best.

EXTENDING THE PLEASURE

With cut flowers, time is always relative, and, equally, pleasure need not be long lasting to be exquisite. You may prefer to spend one day in the presence of a big bowl of short-lived poppies than three weeks with a vase of long-lasting florist's chrysanthemums. It is, however, sensible, once you've made your choice, to get the very freshest flowers, to double, or even triple, the length of your enjoyment.

If the flowers come from your own garden, you should know those which have just opened, and those which have been around a while. You are also in a position to plunge the cut stem or branch, immediately after picking, into water, so there is no risk of the flowers' drying out and wilting. Some experts advocate picking flowers first thing in the morning; others advocate evening picking. In fact, what you do with the flowers after picking is more important than when they are picked. Remove all the flowers and leaves that are going to be below the water line of the container.

Flowers, such as chrysanthemum and rose, which have woody stems, should have the bottom 2.5–5cm (1–2in) of stem hammered or otherwise split. (Some people prefer to scrape the outer bark or skin with a sharp knife; it has much the same effect.) This treatment is also applicable to branches of shrubs and trees.

Some flowers – euphorbias and poppies, for example – release a milky liquid when cut. This can harden and prevent the flower stem drawing up water. The conventional treatment is to dip the stem, immediately after cutting, into boiling water for half a minute or so, or to burn the cut end with a match.

Turn flowers with hollow stems – such as delphiniums and very large dahlias – upside down and fill the stem with water, then stopper with a wad of cotton wool.

Soaking flowers for several hours up to their necks in warm water, then arranging them for display, is a standard procedure among professionals, and does extend the life of the flower. The same treatment is given to foliage, except that it can be submerged in water for a few hours. Evening picking can sensibly be combined with an overnight stay in a water-filled bucket, and the fully turgid plant material can be arranged the next day.

For many people, discussing the fine points of picking garden flowers is totally irrelevant. Instead is a moment's transaction at a flower stall on the way from work; one more pre-wrapped purchase to make during the weekly supermarket.

The practice of pre-wrapping bunches of flowers in opaque paper can hide a multitude of sins, such as slimy, smelly or limp leaves and stems, the prime symptom of floral senility. (Wrapping bunches of flowers in foil-backed paper is very misleading, as well. The reflected flowers, once unwrapped, are far more meagre in reality than they were in image.) It would be unreasonable to open and inspect pre-wrapped flowers before purchase, but do go back and complain if you get a dud lot.

Large chain stores treat cut flowers like fruit and vegetables, and often have 'sell by' dates on the wrapping.

While the stems and leaves may be hidden, the flowers are always open to inspection. Those with pollen visible on the stamens, or as a dust-like yellow covering on the lower petals, means that the flower is on the way out!

Thin-petalled flowers, such as daffodils and scabious, that look dry, papery and translucent, or with dark edges to the petals, are also on the way out. Spiky flowers, such as foxgloves, delphiniums and lupins, die from the bottom up, and a quick inspection should reveal any telltale lower stumps that once held flowers. Flowers with many rows of petals tend to drop their outer petals first and, again, it is worth having a quick close look before buying them.

Fully open flowers have a shorter life than buds, although very tight small buds, without any flower colour showing, may choose not to open at all.

Pre-wrapped flowers, particularly, are held upright and the buds tightly closed only by the pressure of the paper. Once unwrapped, the floral 'lambs' reveal themselves for the mutton they are.

Store-bought flowers benefit from being cut again, about 2cm ($\frac{3}{4}$in) above the original cut, as soon as they are home. Immediately after cutting them, give the flowers a good deep soak in warm water. Lastly, flowers don't just sit in water; they drink it. Inspect the containers frequently and add more water as necessary. Every few days, clean out the container and change the water entirely, recutting slimy stems and removing faded flowers. In warm dry rooms, most flowers benefit from occasional misting with tepid water.

PLANT LISTS

Name Dropping

Every plant has a proper botanical name, which distinguishes it absolutely from other plants, and which is the same in every language. Most plants, however, spend their whole lives without ever being addressed properly, often suffering instead the indignity of confusing common names. Take, for example, the lovely pink-flowered climber, correctly called *Lapageria rosea*. *Lapageria*, its generic name (roughly the biological equivalent of a family surname), commemorates Napoleon Bonaparte's wife, Empress Josephine of France, whose maiden name was de la Pagerie. The specific name, *rosea*, (roughly equivalent to a Christian name) refers to the pink colour of the bell-shaped blooms. It is, however, far more commonly referred to as the Chilean bellflower (or bell flower or bell-flower, depending on the whim of the author or publisher), because it originates from Chile. Because it is a member of the lily family, the plant is sometimes called the climbing lily (a name far more suited to the glory lily), and old-fashioned gardening books refer to it as Napoleon's bell.

When you think that most house plants have at least one common name, often several, some of which might be shared with a quite different plant – *Saxifraga sarmentosa* and *Tolmeia menziesii*, both mother of thousands, spring to mind – you can understand the chaos. Multiply that by the number of common names given to a single plant in different languages, and the mind boggles.

While taxonomists throw up their hands in despair, you can also understand the attraction of common names. Most botanical nomenclature is Latin or Greek in origin, and unless you have a good grounding in the classics, however descriptive the names are in their original language, they are absolutely meaningless. Even those botanical names that are commemorative, such as *Lapageria* or *Fuchsia*, named after Leonard Fuchs, a fourteenth-century German botanist, usually refer to long-dead and now obscure missionaries, personalities or plant hunters active at the time that the plant was discovered or popularized. (The modern-day equivalent is probably naming new cultivars of roses after television personalities . . .)

Publishers of popular books on gardening don't like botanical names because they are not 'reader friendly' and, frankly, tend to put people off. In terms of pure graphic design, botanical names are conventionally printed in italics, to set them apart from the text, and the result is often an unpleasant, 'peppery' look to the book, which can be difficult to read. Also, italics can make a book far more erudite in appearance than it actually is.

Those who market house plants on a large scale may not have graphic design in mind, but they certainly make an effort to avoid botanical names. Pre-packed plants sold in petrol station forecourts have their names honed down to the absolute minimum, 'Shrub rose, red' and 'Flowering bulbs' are two desperate examples of what can go wrong with common names. (Both of these signs described totally dormant plants, the latter packaged in opaque wrapping, to stymie even the most knowledgeable gardener!)

In an ideal world, plant labels would wear both common and complete botanical names, and gardening books would have 'conversion' lists in the back, as this one does. Sometimes, the generic name is also the common name: begonia, for example, or chrysanthemum. This can give a false sense of security. There are hundreds of different begonias and chrysanthemums and, while you may see one you like and buy it, if you have a certain one in mind, and set out with only its generic name, you are unlikely to succeed in finding it.

As well as the generic and specific – the first and second names – there are further subdivisions. There are naturally occurring variations in some species; such plants are known as varieties and usually have a third, italic name after their specific name. Cultivated varieties, or cultivars – the majority of popular house plants are cultivars – have their cultivar name last in Roman typeface, surrounded by single quotes. Though it is the third name, it could still be the vital one, telling you, for example, whether it is the dwarf or giant form of a plant. Lastly, hybrids are the result of crossing two different species or varieties. Hybrids rarely breed true from seed, and usually combine the best qualities of each parent.

Any plant tables that convert popular names to botanical ones are bound to be 'gems in the rough'. As well as the endless variation in common names, botanical names are themselves occasionally subject to change and dispute. A name that was correct two years ago could be incorrect now; one that is correct now could be changed two years' hence. That having been said, the tables should prove helpful if you wish to chase up more information about any of the house plants mentioned in this book, or even buy the plants themselves.

Common	Linnaean	Common	Linnaean	Common	Linnaean
Achimines	*Achimines erecta*	Boston fern	*Nephrolepis exaltata*	Date palm	*Phoenix dactylifera*
	Achimines grandiflora	Bottle brush	*Callistemon citrinus*	Desert fan palm	*Washingtonia filifera*
	Achimines longiflora	Bougainvillea	*Bougainvillea buttiana*	Devil's ivy	*Scindapsus aureus*
African hemp	*Sparmannia africana*		hybrids		*Scindapsus pictus*
African violet	*Saintpaulia* cv		*Bougainvillea glabra*		'Argyraeus'
Agave	*Agave americana*		hybrids	Donkey's tail	*Sedum morganianum*
	Agave americana	Box elder	*Acer negundo* 'Variegatum'	Dracaena	*Dracaena fragrans*
	'Marginata'	Brassaia	*Brassaia actinophylla*		*Dracaena marginalis*
	Agave filifera		(*Schefflera actinophylla*)	Elephant foot plant	*Beaucarnea recurvata*
	Agave victoriae-reginae		*Browallia speciosa* hybrids	Emerald feather	*Asparagus densiflorus*
Aloe	*Aloe arborescens*		*Browallia viscosa* hybrids		'Sprengeri'
	Aloe brevifolia	Buddhist pine	*Podocarpus macrophyllus*	Eucalyptus	*Eucalyptus globulus*
	Aloe variegata	Bulrush	*Scirpus cernuus*		*Eucalyptus gunnii*
Amaryllis	*Hippeastrum* hybrids	Busy Lizzie	*Impatiens petersiana*		*Eucalyptus niphophila*
Angel's wings	*Caladium hortulanam*		*Impatiens wallerana* hybrids	European fan palm	*Chamaerops humilis*
	hybrids	Butterfly flower	*Schizanthus pinnatus*	Fatshedera	x *Fatshedera lizei*
Anthurium	*Anthurium andraeanum*		hybrids	Fatsia	*Fatsia japonica*
	Anthurium crystallinum	Button fern	*Pellaea rotundifolia*	Ficus	*Ficus benjamina*
	Anthurium scherzanum	Caladium	*Caladium hortulanum*		*Ficus elastica*
Arrow-leaf plant	*Syngonium angustatum*		hybrids		*Ficus lyrata*
	Syngonium podophyllum	Calceolaria	*Calceolaria herbeohybrida*		*Ficus pumila*
Arum lily	*Zantedeschia aethiopica*	Callisia	*Callisia elegans*		*Ficus radicans*
Asparagus fern	*Asparagus densiflorus*		*Callisia fragrans*	Fiddle-leaf fig	*Ficus lyrata*
	'Meyers'	Camellia	*Camellia japonica* cvs	Fish-tail palm	*Caryota mitis*
	Asparagus densiflorus	Cape cowslip	*Lachenalia aloides*		*Caryota urens*
	'Sprengeri'	Cape leadwort	*Plumbago capensis*	Flaming sword	*Vriesea splendens*
	Asparagus falcatus	Cape primrose	*Streptocarpus* hybrids	Florist's fern	*Asparagus setaceus* (*A.*
	Asparagus setaceus	Cathedral bells	*Cobaea scandens*		*plumosus*)
	(*A. plumosus*)	Century plant	*Agave americana*	Foxtail fern	*Asparagus densiflorus*
Aspidistra	*Aspidistra elatior*	Chilean bell flower	*Lapageria rosea*		'Meyers'
Azalea	*Rhododendron indicum*	Chilean jasmine	*Mandevillea suaveolens*	Gardenia	*Gardenia jasminoides*
	hybrids	Chinese fan palm	*Livistona chinensis*	Garland flower	*Hedychium coccineum*
	Rhododenron simsii	Chinese jasmine	*Tracheospermum*		*Hedychium coronarium*
	hybrids		*jasminoides*		*Hedychium gardnerianum*
Baby's tears	*Helxine soleirolii*	Christmas cactus	*Schlumbergia* 'Bridgesii'	Geranium	(see Perlargonium)
Bamboo palm	*Rhapsis excelsa*	Christmas cherry	*Solanum capsicastrum*	Ginger lily	*Hedychium*, as above
Bay	*Laurus nobilis*	Chrysanthemum	*Chrysanthemum frutescens*	Glory lily	*Gloriosa rothschildiana*
Begonia	*Begonia boweri*		*Chrysanthemum morifolium*	Glory pea	*Clianthus puniceus*
	Begonia coccinea	Cineraria	*Senecio cruentus*	Grape ivy	*Cissus rhombifolia*
	Begonia 'Erythrophylla'	Cissus	*Cissus antarctica*	Grapfruit	*Citrus paradisi*
	Begonia masoniana		*Cissus rhombifolia*	Grassy-leaved sweet	
	Begonia metallica	Clianthus	*Clianthus puniceus*	flag	*Acorus gramineus*
	Begonia rex-cultorum	Clivia	*Clivia miniata*		'Variegatus'
	hybrids	Coconut palm	*Microcoelum weddellianum*	Guzmania	*Guzmania lingulata*
	Begonia semperflorens-	Coleus	*Coleus blumei* hybrids	Hart's tongue fern	*Phyllitis scolopendrium*
	cultorum hybrids	Columnea	*Columnea* 'Banksii'	Hearts entangled	*Ceropegia woodii*
	Begonia tuberhybrida		*Columnea microphylla*	Heartleaf	
Bird's nest fern	*Asplenium nidus*	Creeping fig	*Ficus pumila*	philodendron	*Philodendron scandens*
	Nidularium fulgens	Croton	*Codiaeum variegatum*	Hen and chicken fern	*Asplenium bulbiferum*
Black-eyed Susan	*Thunbergia alata*		*pictum* cvs	Heptapleurum	*Heptapleurum arboricola*
Blood lily	*Haemanthus coccineus*	Crystal anthurium	*Anthurium crystallinum*	Holly-leaf fern	*Cyrtomium falcatum*
Blushing bromeliad	*Neoregelia carolinae*	Cyclamen	*Cyclamen persicum*		

Hot water plant	*Achimines erecta*	Palm	*Caryota mitis*	Rubber plant	*Ficus elastica decora*
	Achimines grandiflora		*Caryota urens*	Scarborough lily	*Vallota speciosa*
	Achimines longiflora		*Chamaedorea elegans*	Scented-leaved	
Hoya	*Hoya bella*		*Chamaerops humilis*	geranium	*Pelargonium crispum*
	Hoya carnosa		*Chrysalidocarpus lutescens*		*Pelargonium fragrans*
Hydrangea	*Hydrangea macrophylla*		*Cocos weddeliana*		*Pelargonium quercifolium*
	'Hortensia'		*Howea belmoreana*		*Pelargonium tomentosum*
			Howea forsterana	Schefflera	*Brassaia actinophylla*
Ipomoea	*Ipomoea tricolor*		*Livistona chinensis*	Selaginella	*Selaginella apoda*
Italian bellflower	*Campanula isophylla*		*Microcoelum weddellianum*		*Selaginella kraussiana aurea*
Ivy	*Hedera canariensis* cvs		*Phoenix canariensis*		*Selaginella martensii*
	Hedera colchica cvs		*Phoenix dactylifera*	Senecio	*Senecio cruentus*
	Hedera helix cvs		*Phoenix roebelenii*		*Senecio macroglossus*
Ivy-leaved geranium	*Pelargonium peltatum* cvs		*Rhapis excelsa*		*Senecio mikanioides*
Jacaranda	*Jacaranda acutifolia*		*Rhapis humilis*	Shrimp plant	*Beloperone guttata*
Japanese yew	*Podocarpus macrophyllus*		*Trachycarpus fortunei*	Slipper flower	*Calceolaria herbeohybrida*
Jasmine	*Jasminum polyanthum*		*Washingtonia filifera*	Sparmannia	*Sparmannia africana*
		Parrot's bill	*Clianthus puniceus*	Spanish bayonet	*Yucca aloifolia*
Kangaroo vine	*Cissus antarctica*	Parlour palm	*Chamaedorea elegans*	Spider plant	*Chlorophytum comosum*
Kentia palm	*Howea belmoreana*	Passion flower	*Passiflora caerulea*		*vittatum*
	Howea forsterana	Pelargonium	*Pelargonium crispum*	Stag's horn fern	*Platycerium bifurcatum*
Kumquat	*Fortunella japonica*		*Pelargonium domesticum* cvs	Stephanotis	*Stephanotis floribunda*
Lachenalia	*Lachenalia aloides*		*Pelargonium fragrans*	Swedish ivy	*Plectranthus oertendahlii*
Lady palm	*Rhapis excelsa*		*Pelargonium hortorum* cvs		*Plectranthus australis*
	Rhapis humilis		*Pelargonium peltatum* cvs	Swiss cheese plant	*Monstera deliciosa*
Lemon	*Citrus limon* 'Meyer'		*Pelargonium quercifolium*	Sword fern	*Nephrolepis exaltata*
Loquat	*Eriobotrya japonica*		*Pelargonium tomentosum*		
Lobster claw	*Clianthus puniceus*	Peperomia	*Peperomia argyreia*	Tillandsia	*Tillandsia lindenii*
Madagascar periwinkle	*Catharanthus roseus*		*Peperomia caperata*	Trailing geranium	*Pelargonium peltatum* cvs
Marguerite	*Chrysanthemum frutescens*		*Peperomia obtusifolia*	Tuberous-rooted	
Medinella	*Medinella magnifica*		*Peperomia scandens*	begonia	*Begonia tuberhybrida*
Mimosa	*Acacia dealbata*	Philodendron	*Philodendron bipinnatifidum*	Umbrella plant	*Cyperus alternifolius*
Mind-your-own-			*Philodendron* 'Burgundy'	Umbrella tree	*Brassaia actinophylla*
business	*Helxine soleirolii*		*Philodendron scandens*	Urn plant	*Aechmea fasciata*
Minature wax plant	*Hoya bella*		*Philodendron selloum*		
Monstera	*Monstera deliciosa*	Pineapple	*Ananas bracteatus striatus*	Vriesea	*Vriesea fenestralis*
Mother-in-law's			*Ananas comosus variegatus*		*Vriesea splendens*
tongue	*Sansevieria trifasciata* cvs	Pineapple flower	*Eucomis bicolor*	Wandering Jew	*Tradescantia albiflora* cvs
Mother of thousands	*Saxifraga sarmentosa*	Pittosporum	*Pittosporum tenuifolium*		*Tradescantia blossfeldiana*
	Tolmeia menziesii		*Pittosporum tobira*		*variegata*
Myrtle	*Myrtus communis*	Poinsettia	*Euphorbia pulcherrima*		*Tradescantia fluminensis* cvs
		Polyanthus	*Primula* x *polyantha*		*Zebrina pendula*
Napoleon's bell	*Lapageria rosea*	Poor man's orchid	*Schizanthus pinnatus*	Wax begonia	*Begonia semperflorens*
Oleander	*Nerium oleander*		hybrids		*cultorum* hybrids
Orange	*Citrus mitis*	Prayer plant	*Maranta leuconeura*	Wax flower	*Stephanotis floribunda*
Orchid	*Cattleya* spp & cvs	Primrose	*Primula vulgaris*	Wax plant	*Hoya carnosa*
	Cymbidium spp & cvs	Primula	*Primula kewensis*	Weeping fig	*Ficus benjamina*
	Dendrobium spp & cvs		*Primula malacoides*	Windmill palm	*Trachycarpus fortunei*
	Odontoglossum spp & cvs		*Primula obconica*		
	Paphiopedilum spp & cvs		*Primula sinensis*	Yellow palm	*Chrysalidocarpus*
	Phalaenopsis spp & cvs	Purple heart	*Setcreasea purpurea*		*lutescens*
	Vanda spp & cvs	Queen's tears	*Billbergia nutans*	Zebrina	*Zebrina pendula* & cvs
Ornamental capsicum	*Solanum capsicastrum*	Regal pelargonium	*Pelargonium domesticum* cvs	Zonal geraniums	*Pelargonium hortorum* cvs

The publisher thanks the following photographers and organizations for their kind permission to reproduce the photographs in this book:

Heather Angel 111; Guy Bouchet 42, 60, 102, 105; Michael Boys 6–7, 33, 71 (*designer John Stefanidis*) 80; Linda Burgess 113; Camera Press 1, 37 below, 58, 65, 88, 108, 109; Cent Idées (*Maltaverne/Faver*) 48–49, 49 (*Clergironnet*) 62–63, 63, 122–123; Gilles de Chabaneix 18–19, 24, 29, 47, 50, 54–55, 70, 91; Luc de Champris for Maison Française (*Anne Marie Beretta*) 13, 94; Inge Espen-Hansen 118; Good Housekeeping (*Jan Baldwin*) 38–39 (*David Brittain*) 88–89 (*Di Lewis*) 98; Susan Griggs Agency/Michael Boys 117; Lars Hallen 92–93; Jerry Harpur 112; Annet Held 26–27, 84–85, 100–101, 121; Marijke Heuff 76, 116; Neil Holmes 107; Jacqui Hurst 81; Georges Lévêque 66, 75, 106–107; Maison Française (*Gervais*) 31, 45 left, 97 (*Primois*) 82–83 (*Marianne Haas*) 104; La Maison de Marie Claire (*Pataut/Bayle*) 8, 40–41, 57 (*Pataut/Puech*) 10–11 (*Pataut Lautier*) 14–15, 114 (*Hussenot/Hourdin*) 22–23 (*Girandeau/Hirsch-Marie*) 25 below, 27, 37 above, 45 right, 86–87 (*Hussenot*) 28 (*Rozès/Hirsch-Marie*) 30, 32 (*Dirand*) 46 (*Chabaneix/Charbonnier*) 68–69 (*Chabaneix/Puech*) 99; Mon Jardin et Ma Maison (*Yves Duronsoy*) 41 (*Yves Duronsoy/M Broussaud*) 51 (*Nicolas Peron*) 59 (*Nicolas Peron/M Broussaud*) 79 below; Photos Horticultural 56; designer Andrée Putnam 18; Bent Rej 20–21, 60–61, 72, 74, 79 above, 83; Top Agence (*Roland Beaufre*) 115 (*J P Hagnauer, Paris*) 120; Deidi von Schaewen 72–73; Elizabeth Whiting & Associates (*Clive Helm*) 90, 110–111 (*Frank Herholdt*) 34; World of Interiors (*Clive Frost*) 96 (*James Mortimer*) 25 above (*John Vaughan*) 87 (*Fritz von der Schulenburg*) 9.

The following photographs were taken especially for Conran Octopus:

Simon Brown (*François Gilles from I.P.L. Interiors*) 52–53 (*Clifton Nurseries*) 77 (*Nicola Gresswell*) 136; Ken Kirkwood 16, 95.